The Inner Life
of the Counselor

The Inner Life of the Counselor

Robert J. Wicks

WILEY

John Wiley & Sons, Inc.

Copyright © 2012 by John Wiley & Sons, Inc. All rights reserved.

Published by John Wiley & Sons, Inc., Hoboken, New Jersey.

Published simultaneously in Canada.

Library of Congress Cataloging-in-Publication Data:

Wicks, Robert J.

    The inner life of the counselor / Robert J. Wicks.

      p. cm.

    Includes bibliographical references and index.

    ISBN 978-1-118-19374-7 (hardback); ISBN 978-1-118-22762-6 (ebk)

    ISBN 978-1-118-23340-5 (ebk); ISBN 978-1-118-26526-0 (ebk)

      1. Mental health personnel—Life skills guides.   2. Mental health personnel—Job stress.

      3. Mental health personnel and patient. I. Title.

RC440.8.W53   2012

616.89—dc23

                                                   2012008101

Printed in the United States of America

10 9 8 7 6 5 4 3 2 1

For Dan Boyd, Geraldine Fialkowski, Brendan Geary, Eugene Hasson, J. Shep Jeffreys, Michaele Kulick, John McLaughlin, Rick Parsons, and Tom Rodgerson. All consummate clinicians, wonderful human beings, and faithful friends

Contents

In That Place of Sanity: The Inner Life of the Counselor

A Brief Introduction

A psychiatrist's wife once questioned him about the reason for his loyalty to his mentor, the Zen master, Shunryu Suzuki. She wondered why he was so faithful to the guidance he was receiving. He responded by saying, "Where he is, is where I want to be, in that place of sanity" (Chadwick, 1999, p. 313). The "place" he speaks about is where all counselors, therapists, and both professional and nonprofessional caregivers wish to be—not only for themselves, but also so they are able to invite others into this space.

In order for this to happen, as *counselors** we must first take basic steps to encourage resiliency. This includes such activities as self-care, stress management, and those other elements that encourage continued personal growth and professional development. Yet, those who live rich lives as guides and caregivers have realized there is more to a counselor's life than remaining resilient—as important as that is. There is the *gestalt* of the core elements responsible for the way through which all of the counselor's daily and professional encounters are experienced—what we may call here *the inner life*, a "place" that should be explored and nourished through the understanding and practice of mindfulness.

---

*I will use the generic term *counselor* to refer to all psychotherapists and caregivers—be they professional or not.

How we encounter life, *our* life, as well as the intense experiences and needs of others, determines whether we will deepen, remain stagnant, or simply become disillusioned as persons and helpers. As I have maintained and noted elsewhere (*The Resilient Clinician*, Oxford University Press, 2008; and *Riding the Dragon*, Sorin Books, 2003), it is not the amount of darkness in the world that matters. It is not even the amount of darkness in *ourselves* that matters. Instead, in the end, it is how we stand in that very darkness that makes the ultimate difference in how peaceful, joyful, grateful, and satisfied we will be both professionally and personally in life.

In the last several years the topic of "mindfulness" has received expanded attention from us as counselors. In addition, over the past decade, the positive psychology movement fostered by Csikszentmihalyi (1990), Fredrickson (2002), Seligman (2002), and others has helped us see that we need to shift our angle of vision to help our clients (and ourselves, for that matter) to experience greater balance and fullness in life. However, long before these two psychological movements arrived on the scene, the wisdom literature of world spiritualities (albeit usually not always in an empirical way) was addressing the question of how we can live more meaningfully, mindfully, and fully.

In this book, with a focus specifically on the counselor, I wish to tap into some of this classical and contemporary spiritual and psychological wisdom to provide encouragement to professional helpers—in what I believe to be simple, profound ways—to take note of their lives more gently and clearly. The goal is to help them to:

- Let go more readily of the nonessential or destructive.
- Instill a greater sense of mindfulness.

- Fully embrace through practice those elements that can enhance maintaining a healthier perspective—no matter what darkness is being faced in one's clinical practice or personal life.

To encourage a lifelong journey steeped in this wisdom, a list of recommended readings and an opportunity to retreat and reflect on the thoughts of modern mentors of alonetime are also provided at the book's conclusion.

Counseling is both a very challenging and rewarding way to live one's life. (There may be equally meaningful ways to live but, to my mind, certainly none better.) And so, to strengthen the interior life of the counselor is not only a sensible act for helpers, but it is a true act of generosity for those they serve as well.

Each chapter is fairly brief by design. It can be read in the morning so as to be kept midbrain or centered in one's heart as the day unfolds. It also can be pondered as part of the day's review if evening is a better time. The importance is to take the renewal step of reading, reflecting on, and letting this information lead to healthy changes.

Life passes too quickly, so delaying the process of reflection encouraged in this book is dangerous. A spiritual leader once said that one of the most dangerous illusions is to believe you still have time. An Orthodox Jewish Rabbi (who is also a counselor) once led his congregation in reflection during Yom Kippur by handing out to each of those present a small piece of paper with the words "It's later than you think!" on one side and the words "It's never too late!" on the other. That captures the sentiment behind this book. Fortunately, you have time *now* if you take it *now*.

With this in mind, before you begin reading and reflecting on the following short essays on the inner life, let me set the stage for your encounter with the themes to follow by selecting a favorite quote of mine from the contemporary classic, *Wherever You Go, There You Are*, by Jon Kabat-Zinn (1994):

> If what happens now does influence what happens next, then doesn't it make sense to look around a bit from time to time so that you are more in touch with what is happening now, so that you can take your inner and outer bearings and perceive with clarity the path that you are actually on and the direction in which you are going? . . .
>
> It is all too easy to remain on something of a fog-enshrouded, slippery slope right into our graves; or in the fog-dispelling clarity which on occasion precedes the moment of death, to wake up and realize that what we had thought all those years about how life was to be lived and what was important were at best unexamined half-truths based on fear or ignorance, only our own life-limiting ideas and not the truth or the way our life had to be at all.
>
> No one else can do this job of waking up for us, although our family and friends do sometimes try desperately to get through to us, to help us see more clearly or break out of our own blindness. But waking up is ultimately something that each one of us can only do for ourselves. When it comes down to it, wherever *you* go, there *you* are. It's *your* life that is unfolding. (pp. xvi, xvii)

As persons who provide clarity and encouragement as part of their professional identity, counselors should take this admonition as much, if not more, to heart given their work with others. Accordingly, *The Inner Life of the Counselor* will deal with a crucial topic for clinicians: their own sense of self and how they are (and are *not*) living a personally and professionally meaningful, mindful life. As Jon Kabat-Zinn points out, since it is *your* life, what can be more important than that?

AUTHOR'S NOTE

When people pick up a book on mindfulness or "the inner life," they often do so hoping to receive guidance, find answers. But if the material provided is true to the topic, it will also serve to deepen the questions. My hope is that this book will help make this possible. On first blush, this may seem unsatisfactory because often a book like this is sought when one is tired, discouraged, maybe even disillusioned. Yet, paradoxically, these very questions and negatively labeled feelings have provided the motivation, the "gates" to going deeper.

With this in mind, at the end of each chapter (including this Introduction), a few questions will be offered for reflection during the day or at its end. In this way, the themes presented in the chapter can be made the counselor's own by determining ways they are personally relevant. The questions are also offered to help stir up a personal inner dialogue about what has just been read and to prepare for what will be offered in the remainder of the book.

Inner freedom is not something you get through answers you receive. It is something you live. Like gratitude and humility, you can't seek it directly, but you can "seed" the sources of it within you by examining and making your questions deeper and bigger, so that meaning—rather than the compulsive culture you are often surrounded with—silently suggests how your life might be lived and how you, in turn, can guide others in their journey.

Some Questions to Consider at This Point

- As a counselor you lead a busy, challenging life. Because this is so, what allows you to become centered so a compassionate way of meeting clients, family, and friends can remain strong, fruitful, and instructive for you rather than being merely a source of depletion?

- All counselors, whether they are secular or pastoral in their self-definition, seek meaning in both their personal and professional lives. How do you seek meaning in yours? What do you feel your mission is in counseling and your overall life? If you were to write a personal and professional mission statement, what essential elements would be in it?

CHAPTER

1

Creating Space Within

In Ghana, a community of women have a saying written over the door to their residence, which states "A house is made of stones but a home is built in the hearts of people. Welcome to our home." Reading these words and experiencing the smiles of greeting received when the door opens sets the stage for stress to be set aside for all those who enter. This is the kind of greeting all counselors and caregivers seek to offer those who enter their lives looking for help as well. Yet, for this to occur and actually be a genuine encounter with the client, there must be room *within* the counselor for offering such a welcome; otherwise, interpersonal "space" will be absent or contaminated. In the words of psychologist and spiritual writer Henri Nouwen (1975):

> When we think back to the places where we felt most at home, we quickly see that it was where our hosts gave us the precious freedom to come and go on our own terms and did not claim us for their own needs. Only in a free space can re-creation take place and new life be found. The real host is one who offers that space where we do not have to be afraid and where we can listen to our own inner voices and find our own personal way of being human. But to be such a host we have to first of all be at home in our own house. (pp. 72–73)

1

In a similar vein, David Brazier, author of *Zen Therapy* (1995), reminds those in the helping professions that "The therapist models stillness and is not frightened by the client nor what they present. The client feels driven, but the therapist demonstrates that this is not inevitable" (p. 61). A sense of presence and mindfulness on the part of the counselor allows this to be possible. Yet, while creating this space through being mindful is quite simple and powerful, it is not easy—even if we as counselors proclaim our commitment to such an approach to counseling and life.

I remember what I found to be a typical and humorous experience for me on this reality. I had just finished reading a section of a quite informative book on mindfulness and psychotherapy by Germer, Siegel, and Fulton (2005). As I was preparing dinner, the key concept of the book kept coming back to me: Be in the present moment with a true sense of openness. As I was recalling this valuable lesson, I was also in the process of placing my dinner in the oven to be cooked. I was so enthralled with the *concept* of mindfulness that they were encouraging that I was distracted from what I was actually doing and abruptly burnt my hand on the hot rack in the oven. So much for really being truly mindful!

AUTHENTICITY AND TRANSPARENCY

What we request and expect of others, we must be faithful to in ourselves. A young pastoral counselor put it this way:

> The Zulu tribe's most common greeting is *Sawubona*, which translates, "I see you." The response, *Ngikhona*, translates, "I am here." It is our relationships where we are liberated, when we are truly seen through the mirror of another. Pastoral counseling is saying intently to a client, "I see you." Going into a client's inner landscape

with her is based on her trust. I believe this trust is built through relating *Sawubona* to the client. Truly seeing a client and maintaining unconditional appreciation opens the door to a strong therapeutic alliance that fosters trust. Within this context of trust, the client is able to go into her inner landscape, look about, and say, *Sawubona,* "I see you."

However, this same counselor realizes that for this process to take place, it must constantly be taking place in her as well. She goes on to say:

I recently saw a cartoon depicting Socrates, in robe and sandals, holding a sign that states "Know Thyself." A man with a blank stare replies, "How boring." Today's culture is virtually swimming in self-help books, promising fulfillment and happiness and, in the midst of the deluge, it seems the simple, deep truth of the Greek aphorism *gnothi seauton* (know thyself) has either been lost, or has been watered down into 12 easy steps.

What has been remarkable to me, as I have gained counseling experience over the past 2 years, is how little clients know of themselves. And what has been even more remarkable to discover, is how very little I know of myself. This has led me to view my inner landscape as a territory, partially discovered, partially untouched land. Some of the territory I enjoy and cultivate well. It has been weeded and pruned, and is a comfortable place. Some of the land is wholly untended, and it is my instinct to avoid the uncomfortable thoughts, emotions, and beliefs that the land evokes. However, when I do find myself in that territory (and it often happens by surprise), if I can stick around long enough to do a little weeding and pruning, it eventually becomes a peaceful place to dwell.

No one is immune to forgetting their value and need, even those whose life is outwardly committed to being informally mindful (being present, open, and aware), and are involved in the practice of daily formal meditation. This can be especially true when in a caregiving role. An example of this comes to mind when I think of my time working with the English-speaking helpers in Cambodia who were trying to help the Khmer people rebuild their country after years of terror and torture.

Following a presentation to a group of relief workers and NGOs (persons from nongovernmental organizations), an American Buddhist who was working there at the time asked to meet with me privately. She said she was worried about a young Khmer Buddhist who was helping in a local hospital with those persons who had lost limbs from stepping on mines while farming.

Many of the mines placed by different factions during the Cambodian conflict were cleared by the United States Special Forces after the conflict. However, some of the mines were made of plastic, so when the flooding season came, mines from unclear areas sometimes floated into previously cleared areas, and then when the unsuspecting farmers went back into the rice paddies with the assurance it was safe, they would sometimes step on a mine and lose either one or both of their legs.

In the hospital and afterward, the Society of Friends (the Quakers) attempted to deal with this situation by setting up a system in which the patients could be fitted with prosthetic devices so they could walk and be active again. However, before this process took place, the Khmers who had undergone this tragedy would naturally suffer both psychologically and physically. It was during this phase of their recovery that this young Buddhist would visit and console them. His mentor told me that experiencing this suffering day-after-day was very upsetting to him, and he was becoming depressed. It was starting to take a real psychological toll on him, and she was worried about him developing vicarious posttraumatic stress disorder.

When I asked her how he was doing processing the aftermath of such an experience in a brief meditative period, before he returned home, she looked at me with a blank expression and said, "Why, I never thought of having him do that." I then suggested that she have him begin this exploratory process to see how it would help and also suggested other procedures with her on self-care, personal debriefing, the use of mentoring, and other processes of regaining perspective.

Each day we must consciously seek to be mindful and have brief—as well as hopefully longer—meditative periods of formal mindfulness so there is space within us as well as space for others. When I work with physicians and nurses, I use the parallel of the medical model to bring this point across. I let them know that the hospital or health care facility is one of the few places where employees are encouraged to wash their hands not only *after* they go to the bathroom so they don't run the risk of contaminating others but also *before* they go to the bathroom, so they don't run the risk of contaminating themselves with the infections of the patients with whom they have just been in contact.

As counselors, psychologically, and some may say spiritually, it is essential to have space:

- *Before you begin your clinical practice each day* so that you are centered before beginning to see your counseling clients or therapy patients

- *Between clients* so you don't contaminate your next client with the issues of the last one
- *Once your day of consultations is done* so you don't contaminate your family at home or remain absorbed with the negativity you may have experienced during the day

Having such spaces of time to accomplish this is not a nicety; it is a necessity. Otherwise, slowly but surely the insidious depletion of energy and the destruction of a healthy perspective will start to take place. Chronic secondary stress (what some would refer to as "burnout") can be like psychological carbon monoxide poisoning or undergoing a slow, quiet reverse spiritual transfusion. Without knowing it, you become drained, lose the original sense of meaning and mission that counseling reflects and should be, and the negative or stressful aspects of clinical practice become more pronounced while the positive realities of the work lose parity. And so, taking various steps back, each day, is essential—especially for counselors.

Still, knowing this and actually practicing it seems so unrealistic for many counselors. This is the first fallacy, point of denial, or cognitive distortion that must be confronted in caring for your inner life as a counselor or caregiver. Once you do this, several key elements involved in stepping back from the "drivenness" of your own life should be honored. This includes valuing the *sincerity* and *humility* that molds an attitude that directly or indirectly opens up space and atrophies unhealthy self-centeredness.

Sincerity is one of the key elements of effective counseling and leading a life of meaning. Even though we read and attend Continuing Education Units (CEUs) to learn new therapeutic techniques—as, of course, we should—somewhere in our consciousness there is a sense of respect for the *person* of the counselor and some doubt or anxiety about whether we are up to being that person or not.

Fortunately, if such doubts are faced directly, they can become gates to new learning and commitment as well as fresh entryways into deeper awareness for, and sincerity about, what being a counselor truly means. It is also an awakening to what is at the very core of the counseling process: *sincerity*. It is all right at times to feel like a charlatan as a counselor. When we never feel that way, that's when it becomes dangerous. As a matter of fact, when one goes deeper into oneself, feelings of inauthenticity should surface, because while we see the right concept or goal, we recognize we are still far from living it.

Mindfulness meditation, which will be discussed later, helps in this regard, because it enables us to be clearer about our goals and the blocks we put in our way to keep us from reaching them. Many who meditate tell stories of such instances. For example, one counselor educator shared the following experience he had in his office one afternoon.

> I was grappling with something that I needed to address in my own life. If I didn't, I couldn't move on; I would emotionally be frozen in place. Finally, in line with my normal practice at the university and partially out of frustration, I went into my office, closed the door, sat down, and meditated for twenty minutes. As I was doing this, a sense or really a question came to me: Why all this concern about courage to face something in your life? Don't the graduate students you supervise in clinical group have courage to face their issues? Don't the clients who come to you show more courage than you claim that you need now to have to face this issue directly?
>
> When these questions dawned on me, I didn't feel guilt or shame, just clarity. Yes, change or not change, I could with ease face my own personal challenges openly, and when I realized this, I felt free. I felt different.

Humility is also a key, but often an underestimated and unexamined aspect of being a counselor. We seek to help our clients to be extra-ordinary, in other words to be fully themselves. But because much of the impact of this depends on the *presence* of the counselor, it is truly difficult if we as counselors don't recognize deep within ourselves that true ordinariness is tangible wonder and seek it within ourselves as well.

Humility is the ability to fully appreciate our innate gifts and our current "growing edges" in ways that enable us to learn, act, and flow with our lives as never before. Before this important passage we may be drained by defensiveness or wander in our own desert chasing a false image of self that has nothing to do with who we are really meant to be.

Most of us know that at some point we need to go through the gate of humility. That is not the problem. The issue is that we are often unaware of the fact that we have actually stopped being humble and, in the process, have lost our sense of perspective and gratitude. If we are lucky, something wakes us up to this fact, even if rudely. The following story shared with me by a friend illustrates the point quite well:

I had a dream that death
Came the other night,
And Heaven's gate swung wide open.

With kindly grace
An angel ushered me inside;
And there to my astonishment
Stood folks I had known on earth,
And some I had judged
And labeled unfit and of little worth.

Indignant words rose to my lips
But never were set free;
For every face showed stunned surprise,
Not one expected *me*.

—*Anonymous*
(Wicks, 2003, p. 26)

With humility, knowledge is transformed into wisdom. Such wisdom then ultimately leads us to open up new space within ourselves where we, as well as others, can experience true freedom and love. Humility allows us to be transparent; that is why it is so important. So much unnecessary worry and stress can be avoided if we treasure this gift. A dialogue from a collection of classic stories and teachings of the early Christian writers (*Patrologia Latina* and *Patrologia Graeca*) told by the *ammas* (Mothers) and *abbas* (Fathers) of the fourth-century desert in Persia and northern Africa illustrates this. It is told from the vantage point of persons totally dedicated to living a full, meditative life of inner peace, humility, and unself-conscious compassion—a place all of us should seek to be in at some level.

The devil appeared to a Desert Father, in the disguise of an angel of the Lord, and said to him, "I am the angel Gabriel and I have been sent to you."

However, the Father softly responded, "See if you are not being sent to someone else. I certainly do not deserve to have an angel sent to me."

Immediately, the devil disappeared. (Author's translation)

This is the kind of natural attitude we need to have if we wish the perspective, peace, and joy that result when we know and value our ordinary, transparent selves without wasting the energy it takes to add or subtract anything from whom we really are. Humility is an *essential* ingredient in life because it provides a *kenosis*, an emptying of the self. At its core, humility dramatically opens up beautiful space in our inner life that includes:

- A space for simplicity amidst the complex demands of both home and office
- A space for solitude to listen to the messages of our quiet spirit lest they be drowned out by the day's noise
- A space for pacing ourselves while resisting the lure of speed and new technology
- A space for gratefulness and giftedness in a world filled with a sense of entitlement
- A space for honesty and clarity rather than spinning the truth to our own advantage
- A space for real relationships in place of mere manipulation of others
- A space for restraint instead of instant gratification and aggression
- A space for doubt and deeper questions rather than filling ourselves with false certainty and pat answers
- A space for reflection so that compassion doesn't lead to undisciplined activism
- A space for generosity where previously only strident self-interest stood
- A space for transparency where opaque defensiveness is our normal rule
- A space for sound self-respect in lieu of inordinate self-doubt or unbridled self-assurance
- A space for intrigue or curiosity about our actions and motivations so we don't wander down the blind alleys of projection, self-condemnation, or discouragement

- A space for forgiveness so we don't fall prey to rigidity and self-righteousness
- A space for what will always be true rather than solely having an interest in what is currently in vogue
- A space for the courage needed to be ordinary instead of wasting all of our time chasing after what we believe will make us someone special

Yes, the ability to empty ourselves creates new inner space in our lives for the surprising remarkable gifts of humility.

HUMILITY IN SILENCE AND SOLITUDE

Anthony de Mello (1986), an Indian Jesuit priest and psychologist, relates the following classic dialogue between a spiritual master and a novice disciple:

> "Why is everyone here so happy except me?" "Because they have learned to see goodness and beauty everywhere."
>
> "Why don't I see goodness and beauty everywhere?" "Because you cannot see outside of you what you fail to see inside." (p. 35)

When we sit in silence and solitude, we expect a sense of peace. At first, this is what happens. We are so glad that we have entered a space where we are free from the fast pace and tensions of life. However, if we sit long enough we may eventually get uncomfortable, even anxious. We get ideas. We remember things we must do. We want to get up and write these things down, make phone calls, or pick up a book.

If we resist such actions, the next phase of the silent period begins. During this period, we hear the noise that is going on in our belief system. Like a radio turned onto scan, our mind moves from different events—both recent and remote—that have emotional power. Hurts, shame, the silver casket of nostalgia, proud moments, anger, and resentment all come to the surface. Depending on our personality style, we may respond to them with projection, self-condemnation, or discouragement that we are still dealing with these issues and old agendas. This is a crucial point on the road to both humility and a spirit of letting go.

Buddhists would gently suggest that we keep our seat and let the stories of the past move through us, acting as though it were about someone else. No judgment. No excuses. No blame. Just watch. From a Western religious perspective, Amma Syncletica, a fourth-century desert dweller, would also offer encouragement by putting it this way:

> In the beginning of meditation there is struggle and lots of work. . . . But after that, there is indescribable joy. It is just like building a fire: At first it is smoky and your eyes water, but later you get the desired result. Thus we ought to light the divine fire in ourselves with tears and effort. (Author's translation)

From a psychological perspective, what happens in the silence is that we are able to create an opportunity for the irrational but as-yet-undisputed thoughts about ourselves and the world to surface. Such thoughts usually remain in hiding because we don't like them. As soon as they surface, we want to avoid or justify them in some way—even when, maybe especially when, we are alone.

This is unfortunate because they are the front line of deeper irrational beliefs that are crippling us. In therapy, supervision, or spiritual mentoring, we begin to see these irrational beliefs for what they are once we have enough trust to share everything that comes to mind. However, think how wonderful it would be if, in the search for our true selves and the desire to experience the inner space offered by humility, we could also do this *with ourselves* through regular, even brief, periods of silence and solitude.

Lacking opportunities for such uncoverings and debriefings with ourselves, such thoughts are left to attack us at night and keep us awake. They haunt us when events occur in our lives that make us uncomfortable. They pain us when we feel we have done the wrong thing as counselors with clients or in our personal life with family members and friends, or with others in our professional and personal lives who have mistreated us. But such suffering at those times, in those ways, unfortunately doesn't teach us anything of worth. What a waste.

If we intentionally make the space for—in Buddhist imagery—those "unruly children" running around in our unconscious asking to be faced, calmed down, and welcomed home, then our silence and solitude can become a classroom where we learn what is driving us—usually in the *wrong* direction. Also, as was implied by Amma Syncletica in her previous comment, we will have a chance, once the initial dust of delusion settles, to create a space within us to be freer in life and more open to others.

If we see our growing edges clearly—without excuses, inordinate self-blame, or discouragement (maybe because we have not improved quickly enough to our own liking; after all, we are counselors!)—then the energy usually employed to defend (or sometimes unwittingly attack ourselves) can be more profitably understood and channeled into learning how we might better enjoy the life we have been given. In addition, our life, and the way we honestly view it, can provide a clearer path in our counseling and personal relationships as well.

Opening ourselves up to past agendas, distorted thoughts, hurtful ideas, and false beliefs that lurk below the surface, and rise into the vacuum we have created in silence, can teach us much.

We just need to give ourselves the space to allow these unexamined memories and perceptions to surface so we can see, examine, and address them with love and understanding. The brilliant analyst Alfred Adler once pointed out that children are great observers but poor interpreters. The un-worked-through interpretations we also made as children that remain within our unconscious and preconscious are really no different—even though we are counselors and have probably gone through our own therapy as well as intense clinical supervision. We must meet them and allow them to tell their stories if we are to find the truth. Inner freedom is an ongoing process, not a final accomplishment.

Silence and solitude will help us to delve into the joys and darkness in our inner life to accomplish this goal. However, we still cannot find the truth and the freedom of humility by ourselves in quiet meditation, although this is a necessary step in the intriguing process of self-understanding and appreciation. For a fuller self-understanding and appreciation of what humility might mean to us in concrete, practical ways that can be transformative, we will also need direction from the different voices present in our trusted circle of friends who help wake us up, encourage and tease us when we take ourselves too seriously, and inspire us to be all that we can be even though we are where we are at any given point in life (Wicks, 2008).

A true spirit of humility helps us to see our gifts and growing edges with a sense of equanimity. True humility helps us let go of our sense of entitlement, rejoice, and be grateful for all material and personal gifts we have been given in life, especially the gift of who we are. To have such an experience is not narcissism or pride. It's a sense of pure joy to recognize that we've been given intelligence, a sunrise to see, possibly possessing a good disposition, wonderful friends at different points in life, or whatever or whomever we have in our lives for which to be thankful. True humility allows us to enjoy and lift the bushel basket off our talents for everyone in the world to see. We are able to do this without falling into the trap of being an egomaniac, because when we are truly honest about our gifts we also can simultaneously see our growing edges or defensive areas. Our lives become transparent.

In most world spiritualities, there is a wonderful recognition of how we can and should constantly embrace true humility by seeing ourselves directly without a coating of psychological makeup. In essence, we must constantly look at those areas in which we are unfree or defensive. Simultaneously, we must never forget to see and be truly pleased that we are gifted as counselors to be loving people capable of true compassion. (The recent literature on positive psychology certainly points to this need to have a balanced view of ourselves, which includes a clear awareness of our signature strengths.)

After a session of sitting *zazen* (quiet group meditation) with his disciples, Zen Master Shunryu Suzuki put humility's paradoxical quality of being grateful, yet honest, about who we are to them in this way. He said, "You are all perfect as you are." Then, after a short pause, and I suspect with a twinkle in his eye, he quickly added, "But you could all use a little improvement" (Chadwick, 2001, p. 3).

Deep gratefulness and humility go hand in hand because the issue of *quantity*—something valued in a consumer society—falls by the wayside. Instead, with a spirit of "all is gift," the *quality* of so much more around and in us is appreciated. Yet, that gift might seem insignificant without the humility and gratefulness to open our eyes and ears to all that we are given each day.

The senior *dharma* teacher Norman Fischer (2001) puts this simply and unself-consciously in the following experience that he was able to embrace because of the humility and gratefulness he was experiencing at that moment: "Last night I went to sleep. I heard an owl. At that moment I truly didn't need or want anything else for my life, nor did I have the thought that I did not need nor want anything. Just, 'hoot, hoot'" (p. 91).

How often have all of us had small but meaningful experiences such as this and let them slip by? Maybe we have sat inside a warm house wrapped in an oversized sweater when it was a bitterly cold day outside, had a stirring and encouraging conversation with a dear friend, eaten a crisp salad that crunched with each bite, or laughed and had our thoughts twinkle as we read a poem, but still didn't fully recognize these moments for what they were: epiphanies of wonder and awe for which to be grateful.

Sadly, more often than we might be willing to admit, we don't see the daily joys of our counseling practice and life in this way. Like society in general, negative feelings or a sense of distance from our inner selves are our natural spontaneous responses to life. Contrary to this, a spirit of humble gratitude slows us down to recognize the need to pace our lives differently so we can see ourselves, life, and surroundings in a new way. Yet, with space within us and the right attitude or perspective that can arise in the proper use of *alonetime*, we can let go and see that new possibilities can arise in the human psyche no matter how dark things become. Certainly, given our frequent exposure to trauma, loss, depression, and other serious life challenges, this is an important lesson for those of us in the counseling profession to embrace—*now*.

Some Questions to Consider at This Point

> What approaches do you employ to maintain space within yourself so both you and your clients may experience greater freedom?

> What additional steps do you think are realistically possible for you to employ to expand this space within?

What resistances/excuses do you encounter in yourself when you seek periods of silence and solitude?

In your experience, what are some of the most effective ways to "make friends with" these resistances so they will atrophy and allow you to move forward and deeper rather than against or away from these perceived blocks to inner freedom?

CHAPTER

2

Valuing and Accessing Alonetime

Spending time in silence and possibly solitude at the beginning and end of the day, as well as between client contacts, may seem like a luxury for many of us with busy practices, heavy teaching schedules, and involved lives. Yet, even though such realities no doubt exist, taking whatever steps are necessary to incorporate and access such spaces is still a necessity for both quality clinical work and, for that matter, a rich personal life. If we are not to be psychologically contaminated by the darkness or drivenness that people bring into our interpersonal space, we must be able to step back in quiet solitude—not just for reflection, but also to breathe emotionally.

We may not feel as dramatically as authors who feel they must be in total silence for long periods of time or they cannot write. However, as counselors and caregivers, we must have the time and space to recognize, debrief, and free ourselves from the unrealistic negative thinking, unexamined distorted schemas, or countertransferences that may have been stirred up so we don't carry them over into our next therapeutic encounter or bring them back to our families when we return home. Moreover, when we create the space to reflect, meditate, and simply *be*, counseling becomes part of the entire flow of our life—not simply the clinical work we do that stands alongside the rest of our personal life. To accomplish this, one of the initial steps is to intentionally enjoy both the scheduled and unscheduled crumbs of mindfulness in our life, and this process can be logically initiated by how we begin our day.

I used to tease counselors that if in your mind the day ahead was going to be a boring one, an easy way to change all that was to leave home for the clinic, hospital, school, or wherever you work an hour late! The problem is that for some of us this is a regular style of living.

A colleague of mine at a clinic I worked in years ago would always be late—even for meetings she called. She always appeared to be chasing her schedule like a gargoyle on roller skates. Part of her seemed to enjoy this. It made things seem exciting, she always made a dramatic entry, and she seemed to have the feeling because of it that her day was truly filled with many important things and people to whom she needed to attend. Because she was such a lovely person to interact with, people tended to give her the room to do this and simply winked at her behavior, so she didn't have to deal with the negative reactions of others as many of us less gentle persons would. However, this style of behavior started to wear on her as she began to age. She felt the exhaustion more and the unconscious payoffs less. In addition, it became more at odds with her spiritual value system, because she was also a pastoral counselor and valued pacing, mindfulness, and respect for those she was scheduled to be with at a certain time.

Although we may not have this particular style (or at least to this extent), most counselors do feel at certain points that their lives are out of control. The practice is busy. They may be working at several geographic settings. The paperwork seems enormous. Family pressures seem to temporarily be outweighing the joys of relationships at home. Difficult colleagues and extremely demanding clients all seem to be lined up for attention. So, the simple question whose answer may still seem incredibly elusive at the time for them is: How can I find and nourish myself with alonetime and enjoy at least the crumbs of mindfulness as a way to begin to nourish my inner life and, in turn, then have real availability for my family, friends, co-workers, and clients?

ALONETIME

For more than 30 years I have dealt with an unusual type of darkness. When physicians, nurses, or international relief workers found themselves on the edge of burnout; counselors, social workers, or psychologists found themselves losing perspective; or priests confessed to feelings of despair at the abuse crisis in their church, I was often called in to consult, mentor, or present information on the topics of resilience, self-care, and the prevention or limitation of *secondary* stress—the pressures experienced in reaching out to others. The goal in all of these cases was to aid these helping and healing professionals to regain a healthy perspective.

Of all the approaches I offered, the most important one I feel I shared with them is also essential for all of us as counselors to attend to: Namely, how can I better appreciate, expand, and explore the spaces in my life? These inner spaces—when we are physically alone or spending time reflectively within ourselves—are not simply about personal renewal or for the purpose of re-engagement (as important as both of these are). They are about recognizing the scaffolding of expectations that are tyrannizing our lives. Even more importantly, they are also about having a more healthy perspective, being more mindful, and breaking free from the invisible puppeteers in our life that are present when dysfunctional thinking or unrecognized schemas (beliefs) lay unrecognized and unexamined.

Time alone or within ourselves or "alonetime" needs to be appreciated in the broadest sense (not just in the extreme where someone goes off by him- or herself to an isolated spot) in the living opportunities that present themselves during our current normal daily routine. When alonetime is appreciated, explored, and enjoyed in the right way, we can lessen our projections, become easier on ourselves, and not become as discouraged when immediate gratification or success isn't granted. Instead, we may feel a sense of inner ease and intrigue about the life we can live that is before us *right now* rather than constantly being postponed into some uncertain future. As we can see in the following reflection by Peterson (2006), the author of *A Primer in Positive Psychology*, life need not, and *should not*, be postponed—even for apparently practical reasons:

> Like many academics, I spent my young adult years postponing many of the small things that I knew would make me happy, including reading novels for pleasure, learning to cook, taking a photography class, and joining a gym. I would do all of these things when I had time—when I finished school, when I was awarded tenure, and so on. I was fortunate enough to realize that I would never have time unless I made the time. And then the rest of my life began. (p. 22)

Consequently, we need to explore silence and solitude to unearth, appreciate, and fathom the value of such spaces in our life, as a way of ensuring that the rest of our life will be more centered, rich, and renewing. As previously emphasized, this will not simply be a wonderful gift to us, but also to those with whom we relate each day, be it only for a few moments or—as in the case of clients—for a single session or an entire therapy.

Spending time in silence, and possibly at times in solitude, can dramatically affect—for good or for bad—the way we live the rest of our lives. Certain fortunate people have some natural sense of this and say they are attracted to these spaces, whether they be for a few moments or, on occasion, a few days. We can see this even in little children when they step back from being active with others to go and play with their toys by themselves, regroup, and feel once again a sense of inner ease.

When high school counselors report back on the process of a senior retreat, their comments also often echo a shown appreciation for quiet time by adolescents who are used to a daily diet of stimulation. The one thing that most often surprises the adult chaperones, because they are used to dealing with the obvious intensity of young people's lives, is the gratefulness the adolescents express for these silent periods. These times are often rated as the most beneficial and appreciated aspect of the retreat experience, especially when the stage was properly set for these quiet periods.

The same is true for young adults. In an email I received from a friend in The Netherlands, he reported how his spiritual community was trying to support the need for periodic silent spaces that are desired and needed by those entering adulthood today:

> We have a building which is called the *Stiltehuis*—the "House of Silence," where weekends are run to introduce young people to the practice of learning how to be present to self through silence and meditation. A small group have also come together on a regular basis, and there is an interest in creating a community or house for some of these people who are committed to building this into their lives. Some young people come to *Stiltehuis* or the community house for individual time with one of the brothers and a woman who works there. They both

offer individual mentoring. It has been remarkably successful and speaks powerfully of the thirst for a life of the spirit of what is good, renewing, and refreshing among young people.

Adults, as well, demonstrate an appreciation for open moments of silence, the opportunity for some solitude and time to withdraw into themselves to regroup and regain a healthy perspective. These free moments can be captured even when flying on a plane, sitting in a group, or walking down a busy city street. They offer people a chance to take a breath, center themselves, and allow the process of meaning-making to be examined anew so they can see if and how their living is congruent with their hopes. Many adults clearly desire to have the space to be comfortable in their own skin, to have an opportunity to sit with themselves peacefully, to take stock, renew, and achieve a sense of inner ease that translates into the ability to have healthier relationships with themselves and others.

Yet, *how* we seek and approach the spaces in our day and life can make all the difference. The process is not the same as in our search for success in the other areas of our life. From psychologists, writers, contemporary and classic spiritual guides, and secular journeyers, we can see a sampling of what some of those attitudes and approaches might be and how significant periods of solitude and even small crumbs of time spent alone can alter the most intense lives.

Probably no other group has been as articulate as writers and poets have been about the need to be alone so creativity can flourish. Nowhere has this need been more dramatically reflected than in the response of Franz Kafka (1974) to his intended wife. In her letter she said she was looking forward to the time when she could sit and watch him write. After Kafka had time to reflect on this letter, you could tell by the tone and wording of his response that this was quite impossible in his eyes. (As a matter of fact, you could also tell from his words that the subsequent possibility of this marriage, given his "unique personality," was doomed from this point on!)

> You once said that you would like to sit beside me while I write. Listen, in that case I could not write at all. For writing means revealing oneself to excess; that utmost of self-revelation and surrender, in which a human being, when involved with others, would feel he was los-ing himself, and from which, therefore, he will always shrink as long as he is in his right mind—for everyone wants to live as long as he is alive—even the degree of self-revelation and surrender is not enough for writing. Writing that springs from the surface of existence—when there is no other way and the deeper wells have dried up—is nothing, and collapses the moment a truer emo-tion makes that surface shake. That is why one can never be alone enough when one writes, why there can never be enough silence around one when one writes, *why even night is not night enough* (Italics supplied) (pp. 155–156)

Another writer known for his love of silence and solitude is minimalist poet Robert Lax, who spent the last 30 years of his life living alone on Patmos and other Greek Isles. When interviewed by former BBC correspondent Peter France (1996) in his book *Hermits*, Lax's comment on the need for solitude—though much less dramatic—follows the same theme as Kafka's words. Lax says, "I haven't actually consciously looked for solitude. All I've looked for are decent working conditions. I think if I didn't like to write, to do something that works best without interruptions, I might not be so interested in being alone for most of the day" (p. 200). (I might add at this point that the same is the case for counselors, whose work requires periods of quiet if balance and quality therapy is to be truly possible.)

This valuing by Lax of a *place* of solitude in which to create was further explored years later in an interview with him by Steve Gregoriou (2002) in his book entitled *Way of the Dreamcatcher*. In it, he asks Lax why Patmos was so important as an environment of solitude (and a limited form of relationship because Lax did leave his house, so he was not strictly a hermit). Lax replied that the isle of Patmos was important because it offered him:

> A timeless serenity. Generative silence. Awe. The quiet imposed by the volcanic mountains and stones, a real love moving over the face of the waters. In a more familial sense, I did feel like someone might if they had run into their long-lost parents or grandparents— as if everything you've heard in your life, up till then, had just been an echo of something that all along had been planted right here. And the echoes of that something could still be heard. . . . The feeling of sanctuary is quite evident. But I think the island is simply a place where strangers may more easily become friends. . . . [I]t's a wholesome place that naturally fosters self-discovery and genuine *agape*. There's a living tradition here. I felt a great wave of peace when I came to Patmos, and I still sense these peaceful rhythms. (p. 82)

Although few of us could escape to an island, the value of a place where we can be quiet and alone is immeasurable. Writers have much to teach us about the creative power of the place of solitude. Writers and poets such as Rilke (1934) and Thoreau (1853), Grumbach (1994), and Sarton (1973), as well as other artists of the word, can help us appreciate time alone in ways that will encourage us to eke out such spaces in our own schedule and maybe take occasional periods of extended time by ourselves that in the past we might have thought impractical or unnecessary.

Psychologists and psychiatrists also help in the explanation of the value and appropriateness of time spent in silence, solitude, and reflection, even though it is true that they, in the main, have been one of the last groups to recognize and discuss the importance of time spent alone. In possibly his finest work, *Solitude: Returning to the Self*, psychiatrist Anthony Storr (1988) sought to begin rectifying this by noting the lack of appreciation by clinicians—including himself—for periods by oneself. He partially addresses this by citing the early work of psychoanalytic writer Donald Winnicott:

> Modern psychotherapists, including myself, have taken as their criterion of emotional maturity the capacity of the individual to make mature relationships on equal terms. With few exceptions, psychotherapists have omitted to consider the fact that the capacity to be alone is also an aspect of emotional maturity. (p. 18)

One such exception is the psychoanalyst Donald Winnicott. In 1958, Winnicott published a paper on "The Capacity to be Alone," which has become a psychoanalytic classic. Winnicott wrote:

> It is probably true to say that in psycho-analytic literature more has been written on the *fear* of being alone or *wish* to be alone than on the *ability* to be alone; also a considerable amount of work has been done on the withdrawn state, a defensive organization implying an expectation of persecution. It would seem to me that

a discussion of the *positive* aspects of the capacity to be alone is overdue. (p. 18)

Following Storr, psychologist Estes Schuler Buchholtz (1997) published a book-length work *The Call of Solitude: Alonetime in a World of Attachment*. In it she also made the point that a balance is needed between being alone and in relationship. She wrote: "We are born wanting and needing time and space alone to process the stimulation around us, as we also learn quickly to revel in and long for attached and related times" (p. 49).

From a developmental standpoint, psychologist Barbara Powell (1985) pointed as well to the longstanding value solitude has for many cultures:

> In many societies, voluntary isolation from others is considered necessary for the completion of certain phases of personal growth. Adolescent males entering adulthood in certain tribal cultures are expected to wander alone in the forest, mountains, or desert for as long as several months at a time. During this period the solitary wanderer is instructed to communicate with the [divine], compose a song, or experience a magic dream. Those who return without their dream may be sent back into the mountains and told to return when they are successful. (p. 35)

Following this, time in silence—and possibly solitude—was also emphasized in writings on mindfulness meditation. This information looked at formal alonetime as meditation in which persons could fruitfully spend time within themselves. Such writings by psychologists and psychiatrists also expressed the value of informal mindfulness as an ideal psychological and/or spiritual partner (depending on how you view this process) during daily activities. In terms of mindfulness meditation, Christopher Germer (2005) notes:

> [Mindfulness] can be compared to a *searchlight* that illumines a wider range of objects as they arise in awareness, one at a time. The benefits are greater awareness of the personal condition of our minds and an understanding of the nature of mind itself. . . . Mindfulness meditation helps us to develop the capacity for relaxed, choiceless awareness in which conscious attention moves instantly and naturally among the changing elements of experience. . . . Meditation can be practiced sitting, standing, lying down, or moving. Mindfulness meditation is not hard to learn; and anyone can practice it. (pp. 15–16)

The psychology of meditation now has much to offer us on the need for, and dynamics of, spending time alone as well as—in Germer's words again—"[developing] a skill that allows us to be less reactive to what is happening in the moment. [Mindfulness] is a way of relating to *all* experience—positive, negative, and neutral—such that our overall level of suffering is reduced and our sense of well-being increases" (p. 4). Given this, being familiar with both formal mindfulness (meditation) and informal mindfulness (being attentive and open in the moment) can significantly enhance our well-being.

Many classic and contemporary spiritual figures have also been proponents of spending time quietly and reflectively, whether individually or in groups. Christian spirituality, for instance, has an established history of prizing leaning back from the bustle of activity. This tradition sees that time alone not only provides an opportunity for refreshment and renewal but also is necessary so we can find our true identity. Kenneth Leech (1985) traces this appreciation of solitude in his book *Experiencing God* in the following way:

> Elijah, who journeyed into the desert for forty days and forty nights, and, arriving at Horeb, lodged in a cave . . . has been seen as a key figure for those seeking God in solitude and stillness. . . . Jesus too was led by the spirit in the wilderness where he experienced temptations . . . and throughout his ministry he is described as having sought solitude in deserts and lonely places, instructing his disciples to follow his example. . . . In the New Testament, the Judean wilderness was the context for the preaching of John the Baptist, identified as 'a voice crying in the wilderness.' . . . The desert experience was one with which the early Christians too were familiar, for they saw themselves as a pilgrim people seeking a better country. . . . The sense of belonging nowhere, of having no continuing city, is one which comes across powerfully in the literature of early Christians. (pp. 129–130)

Included in this group of early Christians who sought solitude were the fourth-century women (*Ammas*) and men (*Abbas*) who fled to the desert to find and preserve their true identities. In the following realistic but challenging words of Trappist contemplative Thomas Merton (1960) about these desert *Ammas* and *Abbas*, we can see their journey is valued to this day by those who wish to be true to themselves and become persons who hold fast to serious values:

> We cannot do exactly what they did. But we must be as thorough and as ruthless in our determination to break

all spiritual chains, and cast off the domination of alien compulsions, to find our true selves, to discover and develop our inalienable spiritual liberty and use it. . . . Let it suffice for me to say that we need to learn from these [persons] of the fourth century how to ignore prejudice, defy compulsion and strike out fearlessly into the unknown. (p. 24)

Psychologist and spiritual writer Henri Nouwen (1981) also valued these desert dwellers and wrote *Way of the Heart* to encourage his contemporaries to value both solitude and silence. To his fellow spiritual seekers he wrote:

In solitude I get rid of my scaffolding. . . . It is this nothingness that I have to face in my solitude, a nothingness so dreaded that everything in me wants to run to my friends, my work, and my distractions so that I can forget my nothingness and make myself believe that I am worth something. (p. 27)

He then adds about silence: "Silence completes and intensifies solitude. . . . [It] protects the inner fire" (p. 43).

Jewish spiritual guides also address alonetime. Abraham Joshua Heschel's (1951) book *The Sabbath: Its Meaning for Modern Man* does so eloquently by encouraging weekly separation from the daily grind of our work week. (What I refer to as "alonetime" may not simply be separation from other people but from a way of existence and a habitual style of interacting that can be destructive if it goes uninterrupted or is not broken up.)

In *The Sabbath* he notes, "In the tempestuous ocean of time and toil there are islands of stillness where man may enter a harbor and reclaim his dignity. The island is the seventh day, the

Sabbath, a day of detachment from things, instruments, and practical affairs" (p. 29).

Orthodox rabbi Aryeh Kaplan (1982), on the other hand, addresses a more formal type of time spent in silence: meditation. In his book *Meditation and Kabbalah*, he goes out of his way to tie meditation to several sources, indicating the later 18th century and early 19th century as its most popular period in Judaism. He also acknowledges the fact that the techniques used are similar throughout the different world religions, and he points out that in Judaism there is often a lack of awareness of this tradition of meditation among practicing Jews:

> With the spread of the Hasidic movement in the Eighteenth Century, a number of meditative techniques became more popular, especially those centered around the formal prayer service. This reached its zenith in the teachings of Rabbi Nachman of Breslov (1772–1810), who discusses meditation in considerable length. Many people express surprise that the Jewish tradition contains a formal meditative system. (p. 3)

Exploring the work of Kaplan then is very revealing, as is further examining the writings of Heschel, who will draw upon past figures who knew how to distance themselves from everyday activity. They were also open to renewing, reflective time to the extent that it is defined not just as time in solitude but also time *within* oneself.

It is no surprise that contemporary Buddhist and Zen masters also value time in quiet reflection as well. Pico Iyer (2008), in his book on the Dalai Lama, noted that "his public virtues were really just symptoms of the private practices and stillness that underlay them" (p. 58). This is not surprising, because from a Buddhist perspective, practitioner's enemies are internal ones: ignorance, anger, attachment, and pride. In this respect then, time alone in meditation or performing a spiritual ritual is not simply something to add on to an already overbooked schedule but something that will make it and your life more meaningful.

According to Sandy Johnson (1996) in *The Book of Tibetan Elders*, "Shambala," which has been portrayed in both novel and movie as an exotic place of peace and joy, is really seen as a "metaphor for one's own inner spiritual journey and [many Tibetans] dedicate their lives to finding it within themselves" (p. 5). In this regard, time alone allows people to examine their minds, see their behaviors and intentions for what they truly and totally are, so they can refocus on what is both growthful and compassionate.

So, for the Buddhist then, alonetime has a purpose. In the words of one of the leading contemporary American spokespersons for Buddhist spirituality (who is also a psychologist), Jack Kornfield (2000) states:

> We live in disordered times, complicated, distracted, and demanding, yet to sustain a spiritual practice demands our steady attention. The first task, then, in almost any spiritual voyage, is to quiet ourselves enough to listen to the voices of our hearts, to listen to that which is beyond our daily affairs. Whether in prayer or meditation, in visualization, fasting, or song, we need to step out of our usual roles, out of the busy days on automatic pilot. We need to find a way to become receptive and open. (p. 25)

Kornfield then broadens the value of alonetime beyond the Buddhist tradition to point out that most major religions and philosophies value being apart, and follows this with a recognition of the potential challenges this can offer:

> In entering solitude one does not necessarily find silence. At first solitude can be noisy, filled with the conflicts of the body and the mind's ongoing commentary that Chogyam Trungpa called "subconscious gossip." Meditation practices help us to find a way to genuine stillness. In them we find that there are many levels to silence. The first is simply external silence, and absence of noise. Then there is the silence of the body, a growing physical stillness. Gradually there comes a quieting of the mind. Then we discover the silence that comes as witness to all things, and then twenty other levels of silent absorption in prayer and meditation. Still deeper we come to the indescribable silence beyond the mind, the silence that gives birth to all things. To enter silence is a journey, a letting go into progressively more profound levels of stillness until we disappear in the vastness. (p. 83)

Consequently, Buddhism, as well as Jewish, Christian, and other world spiritualities, seems to have much to offer in appreciating the value and challenges of silence, solitude, and time alone—whether we are religious or not.

There are also numerous, what I would term, "secular adventurers" in the exploration and appreciation of quiet time alone or with others. They help us appreciate that silence and solitude can sometimes seem like a different world to us when we experience it in the extreme. Gertrude Bell, ally of Lawrence of Arabia, noted having this experience in a letter to her father.

In commenting on one of her encounters with the desert, she wrote to him:

> Shall I tell you my chief impression [of the desert]—the silence. It is like the silence of mountain tops, but more intense, for there you know the sound of wind and far-away water and falling ice and stone; there is a sort of echo there, you know it, Father. But here *nothing*. (Italics supplied, Wallach, 1996, p. 54)

Bell is one of the many secular searchers and adventurers who have experienced the power of silence, possibly at times along with solitude. There are many others who join her—some with a more intentional sense of spending time in meditation or being with others with a deep sense of presence and awareness—in other words, "mindfulness." One of the most recent such practitioners is Clark Strand (1988), a former Buddhist monk. In his book *The Wooden Bowl* he sets out the desire for, and response to, formal periods of being alone or meditation.

He began this book by explaining his former commitment to Buddhism and his subsequent mindful practices when alone after leaving participation in this way of life as a leader in his temple. He then poses the question: "Was there a way for people to slow down and experience themselves, their lives, and other people in the present moment without adopting a new religion or philosophical ideology?" (p. 2). He felt that if it were possible it would result in a person maintaining "a spirit of lightness and friendliness with regard to what you are doing" and that meditation "ought to be an area of your life where you can let go of the obsessive desire to improve yourself, to get ahead, or to do better than anyone else. . . . Meditation ought to decrease the drivenness of our lives, not make it worse" (p. 12).

In his encouraging us to spend part of our time alone in meditation, he is asking us to experience "brief glimpses of a freer, more spacious world" (p. 21), whether we meditate briefly for a few moments or an extended period. He believes that through sitting with a comfortably erect posture (after all, meditation is not a rigid "charm school") and through the use of a simple counting procedure (1 to 4) of our breaths, we can remind ourselves to take life as it is and comes to us. (More extensive guidance on meditation—as well as informal mindfulness to complement it for those who don't wish to meditate—will be included later in the book and can also be followed up by sampling the recommended readings on the topic listed at the end of the book.)

Designated times of silence as it is experienced by Strand in formal or informal meditative approaches to life, according to him, are essential if we are to have life and live it abundantly. In his sense of viewing it, a meditative approach to our alonetime will help people see more fully the "fundamental *enoughness, sanity,* and *beauty* of the world" (p. 14).

Less formal in his approach than Strand's to time in silence—but this time with the added element of solitude—are those informal periods that are described by Richard Bode (1993), author of the simple, elegantly written book, *First You Have to Row a Little Boat*. In this book, using sailing as a metaphor for how we appreciate or ignore how life should be lived, he makes the point that we need to learn to make adjustments in life as a sailor tacking his sloop is called to do.

> The truth is that in our daily lives we constantly make similar migrations from land to water and back to land again—and we don't always do so with the fluency of the sailor. Time flips us rapidly from place to place and role to role. We shuttle from suburb to city, from home to job,

from business meeting to dinner party. Each milieu has its own conventions and makes its own demands. Sometimes the changes occur so fast we lose our bearings. We behave like parents to our colleagues and executives to our kids. We lack a sure sense of the appropriate because we haven't taken the time to figure out where we are. (pp. 12–13)

From his time sailing alone, he sees the need for us to have time to breathe, reflect, respect the currents of life, and respond to our hopes rather than inadvertently kill them.

When we kill the dream within us, we kill ourselves, even though the blood continues to flow within our veins. We can see the signs of this living death about us everywhere: in shopping malls, in discount and department stores. . . . We see people scurrying compulsively, buying compulsively, as if they hoped through the expenditure of money, the acquisition of goods, to deaden the pain they don't even know they have. (p. 24)

In addition to his time on his sloop alone, Bode also had an enforced idleness because of an accident. During this time he reflected:

I thought deeply about who I was, where I came from, and what I wanted to be. What I had lost in physical motion I had gained in insight, which is movement of another kind. I learned the interior life was as rewarding as the exterior life and that my richest moments occurred when I was absolutely still. (p. 70)

Bode's simple words typify the experiences and comments of other secular adventurers in alonetime, as well as those from writers, psychologists, and spiritual authors, who show respect for a formal Sabbath and the informal spaces in our lives.

RECOGNIZING, HONORING, AND APPRECIATING MORE FULLY THE SPACES IN DAILY LIFE

As in anything valuable for our welfare and, by natural extension, our clients and the persons who are part of our interpersonal community, time spent in silence, solitude, and some form of formal or informal mindfulness needs to be respected and fully understood if it is to have a positive effect. Otherwise, such spaces in our lives run the risk of being relegated to being no more than useless empty holes within "the real action" of life or simply represent those times when we merely brood about what we may have said to someone or resent what has happened to us yesterday or yesteryear.

Given this, it is essential—*especially* as counselors and caregivers—to address the questions that will help us to uncover and enhance the spaces in our life. To accomplish this goal, some questions need to be addressed, such as: How can time alone and within ourselves become a more fruitful, enlightening, challenging, and renewing place? What pitfalls might we encounter? How can we meet such perils in ways that actually result in their paradoxically being an advantage to us?

The dynamics of enjoying and benefiting more from the spaces one recognizes or creates may hold some surprises since solitude and reflective time are often taken for granted or seen as needing no introduction. The feeling often is, "What's the big deal about being alone? Anyone can step aside or become reflective when in a group." Yet, as psychologists, poets and writers, spiritual figures, and other searchers have recognized, there is so much to learn about time in silence, solitude, and mindful presence. This includes:

- Uncovering the resistances to and reasons for seeking space in our active lives
- Appreciating the expectations we have for time alone and the surprises it can offer us
- Determining how we can make it a priority
- Experiencing how time in silence and solitude can "positively contaminate" the rest of our day
- Knowing the differences between being alone and lonely
- Understanding the simplicity that periods of quiet time can foster in our life
- Recognizing the conduit free time can be for unlearning as well as new learning for us

Part of the goal of nurturing one's inner life is to provide a panoply of approaches to how silence, solitude, and mindfulness can be viewed from different, possibly surprising angles. Free, quiet moments will never again be seen as being merely the interruptions or stopgaps in a life of activity and function. Instead, very brief informal periods and formal lengthy times when we are physically alone or within ourselves (even when surrounded by others) will be something else, something more, something into which we can enter to alter our whole life in some very significant ways.

APPRECIATING THE CRUMBS OF ALONETIME

Alonetime already exists throughout much of our day, no matter how hectic our schedule is. One of the first steps in leaning back so we can capture moments of silence, solitude, and reflection is to recognize them. Crumbs of silence and solitude are easily ignored or swept away. This often results in a vision of being at peace and alone as being in the purview of pure fantasy for most of us. Consequently, while we love to read about a hermit's experience, we let the available spaces in our own day lay unnoticed and unfathomed for what they might be.

If anything then, free time needs to be appreciated first for what it is now in our life—not for what we would like it to be. Just as people would starve if they continued to read extravagant menus or recipes and didn't eat the simple meal before them, so too would their inner lives be starved if they didn't actually experience the quiet, solitude, and a chance to explore their interior terrain that is already available but for some reason is presently being left unnoticed and not fully experienced.

Writer Sara Maitland (2008) recognized this in her search for deeper and broader silence. She wrote,

> One of the things I discovered at this point was that there were bits and pieces of silence woven into the fabric of each day and I began to try to keep an eye out for them and move into them as swiftly as possible. Some of these moments I had to create for myself . . . but some were just *there*, waiting for me. (p. 154)

When we seek small moments of silence and solitude with a sense of fervor, it is a fallacy to think that in doing this we are merely settling for less. Instead, we are moving with our present busy reality in seeking the space that is already available, but being left not fully accessed, to breathe, reflect, renew, learn, and relax—just be. From another perspective, Annie Dillard (1989) recognized how the larger periods begin with a love of the smaller and symbolic moments. In her classic work, *The Writing Life*, she told a story to illustrate this with respect to being a writer:

> A well-known writer got collared by a university student who asked, "Do you think I could be a writer?"
>
> "Well," the writer said, "I don't know. . . . Do you like sentences?"
>
> The writer could see the student's amazement. Sentences? Do I like sentences? I am twenty years old and do I like sentences? If he had liked sentences, of course, he could begin, like a joyful painter I knew. I asked him how he came to be a painter. He said, "I liked the smell of paint?" (p. 70)

Using this approach with the goals for this book in mind, the question is simple then: As a counselor, do you like the crumbs of silence and solitude you already have and can discover? If you do, you can begin to become someone who will enjoy a deep sense of alonetime.

WHAT ARE SOME OF THE CRUMBS OF ALONETIME?

For most of us there are periods in life that are already open. They might include early morning before the rest of the house awakes, at the end of the day after everyone turns in for the night, when driving in the car to and from the clinical practice, when walking to the restroom, the few seconds before answering a ringing cell phone, during a lunchtime walk, while jogging or at the gym, or waiting on a line or in a doctor's or dentist's office. It may be an even longer period of time, such as when one is home alone or during a scheduled day of renewal.

As counselors we also have additional built-in opportunities for alonetime (though for some reason we may not recognize them as such). They include:

- Client cancellations
- Quiet periods before or after client hours
- The space between clients
- Time after attending a CEU event

Client cancellations are perfect times to take 15 minutes to:

- Close the door of the office.
- Sit up in a chair or on a cushion.
- Simply count breaths from 1 to 4.
- Gently look at an object that inspires.
- Simply *be*. How hard can that be?

There are also other times when we can take a nice walk to increase our oxygen exchange and stretch our legs given all the sitting that is part of a clinical practice. During such times a good exercise is to simply look at and experience the surroundings. In this way we are truly taking an energizing walk instead of merely "taking a think"—in other words, walking around, slightly hunched over, pondering things in our life while the experiences of life and all that is around us passes us by while we remain in a psychological envelope of preoccupation and concern. When we are involved in such cognitive self-centered functions, we miss so much. Buddhist Pema Chodron (1997, p. 31) used to refer to such involvement as tantamount to wearing earplugs while walking up to a tree filled with singing birds.

During quiet periods before or after client hours, as well as between each of them, other opportunities are presented to us for a few moments of silence and solitude. In addition to this, another opportunity can present itself if you (a) leave for work a bit earlier so you are not racing to see the first client in your practice; (b) close your door so no one comes to chat; and (c) take a few breaths before the intensity of counseling begins. This allows us then to be mindful (alert, present, and open) to the first client *and* the day. Otherwise, we run the risk of contaminating the first session and the rest of the day with elements involved in our home life. Moreover, not having a space before and between sessions also increases the chances that we will be less open to what is actually happening to the client in the room and causing us to rely more on the diagnostic box in which we may have placed the client.

Time after a CEU is another one of many periods that counselors have to not only digest what they have learned but also to lean back and relax with the cognitive input received. This allows us to be open to all that lies below and beyond our thought processes and analytic skills. There is more to us than the cognitive aspect, so why not enjoy that part of ourselves as well?

Small crumbs of silence and solitude when they are recognized and enjoyed do two things: (1) they help nourish us immediately and (2) they inspire and call us to seek more and lengthier periods of alonetime. When this happens we can then see how such periods bring us to life and help us to feel fresher and more open. We will also begin to more deeply appreciate such important realities as *impermanence* and the *fragility of life*, so we value what little time we have here in the world and in the process respect others who also are here on this earth for a short time. This will also help us see more clearly how often we are mindless, which need not be the source of self-castigation but, instead, can be turned into places where we can profitably attend to in both our professional and personal lives.

Some Questions to Consider at This Point

Where in your life does quiet time already exist?

In what parts of your life is it realistic to create some new space where you can relax and practice mindful breathing?

Imagine people in your life whom you admire because they are more reflective and relaxed than you are. What are some basic ways to emulate them?

In what ways can you create an environment in your home and office that is conducive to sitting meditation and mindful breathing?

How can you develop a list of triggers to help you be mindful so you don't just run to your grave thinking that once this task is done you will take time? (These reminders can and should include common daily triggers such as the ring of a phone, entering your car to drive to work or do an errand, your morning alarm clock, entering the shower, sitting down to a meal, etc.)

How might you create significant time and occasionally a day or longer in which you have nothing on the schedule? (This may require that you leave the house or office, because sitting there may remind you of what you still have left unfinished, but whatever needs to be done to create such a leisure space is worth the effort.)

CHAPTER

3

———◆◇◆———

Recognizing the Cues
of Subtle "Mindlessness"

In the novel *The Second Coming* by writer and physician Walker Percy (1980), one of the characters quips, "What if I missed my life like a person misses a plane?" Well, that is so easy to do in life if—maybe, paradoxically, *especially if*—you spend a great deal of time counseling others.

Nurturing our inner life as counselors involves honoring the *experience* of what is healthy and whole—not simply in increasing our ability to mentally diagnose when life isn't, and in only being able to verbally describe what it should be. Knowing *about* the value of having a less-fractious ego, rather than actually *being* an integrated person without guile, who purifies the psychological air for those she or he encounters, is not sufficient.

Counselors who are open to criticism without being unduly defensive, who experience praise by a colleague as fun—nothing more—and are awake to life as it unfolds in the now are free enough to enjoy the present without being unduly fooled by their predominant familial, professional, or societal culture.

When I *act* like a clinical psychologist my family and friends know it and waste no time letting me know how I am behaving.

Yet, when I truly am a healthy psychologist in how I live, no one minds; they even seem to take heart from the space it offers them.

For a counselor, being analytic is a great gift that should not be surrendered. However, in counseling as in life, such a talent needs to be pruned and balanced so the counselor doesn't think too much and live too little. To do this we must be able to pick up the cues of "mindlessness." Therefore, appreciating the red flags that mark a shift of energy away from being present in the now with an openness to everything that comes our way to a mindlessness marked by unhealthy self-absorption, withdrawal, defense, or distraction is very helpful.

When we recognize when we are starting to behave in mindless ways, we can then simply return to being more present and open by taking a breath, leaning back into the now, and looking to see where new truths or possibilities might be present in what we are encountering. Surprisingly, such awareness may not immediately result in the alleviation of the possibly uncomfortable feelings being experienced at the time. However, it can result in providing the initial space for the development of a new perspective and greater freedom that we previously didn't have under such circumstances to take root.

For instance, it may simply be that as counselors we begin to recognize that a certain type of person who comes in to see us seems to elicit a particular type of unpleasant inner reaction. As well as having diagnostic value, maybe it is also information we need for the next phase of our life rather than simply the next phase of the client's treatment. The result of such awareness is a greater inner space and a freer presence for the clients who subsequently can then see the possibility for greater freedom in their lives as well.

APPRECIATING WAYS TO BE MORE MINDFUL SO WE CAN MORE EASILY RECOGNIZE WHEN WE ARE NOT

Attention to how one can live more mindfully is something that can be taught to clients. In the session, clients are helped to focus a bit more so they can see more clearly their emotions and cognitions as sources of their styles of behavior. Through summarization, for example (which, as we know, is the least intrusive form of interpretation), we simply connect similar events that seem to have the same (often negatively perceived) outcomes and ask them how they understand this and what they make of it. In this way, the less obvious becomes clearer. However, we would become more in tune with doing this with our clients if we also practiced on ourselves.

When we as counselors see and embrace mindfulness in an ongoing way, not only do we benefit, but our clients do as well. For instance, it allows us to be more perceptive concerning what is present in ourselves and others without judgment (which would distract us from seeing clearly), so we can experience situations more fully. Still, to do this, just as in the case of undertaking a practice of structured mindfulness meditation, we must always view ourselves as beginners, learning anew each day.

Each session we have with someone can then be fresh and new. To accomplish this in meditation, we need to approach ourselves with no preconceived notions of what will happen or a gaining idea in our minds. Similarly, in counseling, if we focus on success rather than on professional and personal faithfulness, the session may quickly turn stale because our eye is no longer on the target (being as healthy and compassionate as possible) but is about winning in some form (albeit for a good reason—the benefit of the client). Consequently, recognizing the following types of mindless behavior and attitudes as counselors is a good beginning:

- Getting too easily upset—often over the wrong things (client is late, resistant, wishes to change therapists)—and missing what life is offering us in all interactions and events (an opportunity to learn from our reactions as well as information from outside ourselves)
- Seeing interruptions only as disruptive rather than as informative or possible, unexpected opportunities to see or experience something new or differently
- Possessing habits and rules that continue to sap life's freshness for us
- Spending too much time in the silver casket of nostalgia or rushing through precious moments of our life under the impression that living this way is "only practical" and temporary—though these temporaries can link together to form a lifetime of mindlessness
- Only fantasizing about both "the spirit of simplicity" and "letting go" rather than seeking to instill them more in our own lives in real, concrete ways
- Merely promising to ourselves that we will adopt a healthier lifestyle (developing a sound self-care protocol we will actually follow) in ways that don't ever translate into the necessary actions we need to take on a continual basis
- Like many of our patients/clients, spending so much of the time in a cognitive cocoon of judgment, worry, preoccupation, resentment, fear, and regret that we miss the chance to *experience* life's daily gifts happening all around us
- Having our time in silence and solitude end up being boring and emotionally flat rather than renewing because

we haven't taken the time to learn a few basic lessons in mindfulness

- Ignoring the spiritual gifts of laughter, a child's smile, or a good conversation and instead spending our precious time focusing primarily on increasing such trivial things as fame, power, security, and pleasure

- Not being able to reframe a canceled session, a brief illness, or a delay in our schedule as being a spontaneous opportunity for renewal and educative alonetime

- Being unable or unwilling to see transitions as being as valuable as our destinations even though they make up much of our life

- Not valuing the "ghosts" of our past memories as the teachers of change they can be, but instead merely experiencing them as recollections that pull us down or fill us with regret or resentment

- Failing to appreciate the need for a sense of *intrigue* about ourselves—including both our gifts and growing edges as persons and counselors—while instead having our efforts at self-appreciation overshadowed by (a) projecting faults onto clients or colleagues that we don't see as supportive; (b) inordinate self-blame; or (c) discouragement when we don't succeed as we would like

- Spending too much of our time in running away from what we don't like as well as in "medicating" ourselves, seeking security, or grasping rather than simply enjoying and being grateful for all that is around us

- Rushing around while failing to notice clients or colleagues we have hurt, what we are eating, how we are feeling, or even what we are really doing and supposed to be paying attention to. In other words, failing to appreciate "life in the slow lane" (Norris, 1993, p. 145).

APPRECIATING LIFE IN THE SLOW LANE: SOME ADDITIONAL INSIGHTS FROM PSYCHOLOGISTS, SPIRITUAL FIGURES, WRITERS, AND POETS

"Hurry sickness," psychologist Schalter Buchholtz (1997) recognized in her work *The Call of Solitude*, is the name for "frenzied nonstop, hasty behavior that takes pleasure out of life and can lead to headaches, high blood pressure and heart attacks" (p. 39). To deal with this behavior we must first be willing to see that our lives are sometimes out of control and that we are being quietly led by unrecognized needs and lingering anxieties. Physician and Russian spiritual writer Anthony Bloom (1970) presents this issue quite adeptly in a reflection on a novel by Dickens:

> There is a passage in Dickens' *Pickwick Papers* which is a very good description of my life and probably also of yours. Pickwick goes to the club. He hires a cab and on the way he asks innumerable questions. Among the questions, he says "Tell me, how is it possible that such a mean and miserable horse can drive such a big and heavy cab?" The cabbie replies, "It's not a question of the horse, Sir, it's a question of the wheels," and Pickwick responds, "What do you mean?" And the cabbie answers, "You see we have a magnificent pair of wheels which are so well oiled that it is enough for the horse to stir a little for the wheels to begin to turn and the poor horse must then run for its life." (p. 39)

Bloom then comments, "Take the way in which we live most of the time. We are not the horse that pulls, we are the horse that runs away from the cab in fear of its life" (p. 39). We must see how many unrecognized, distorted thoughts and beliefs have captured our hearts and drive us on, thus taking a toll and making "hurry sickness" seem normal and our frenzied activities seem "practical." As I have noted in a previous chapter, writers—possibly more than we as counselors do—seem to see the value of alonetime—not just for their creative activity but for what underpins what they do and how they live.

May Sarton (1973), American novelist, poet, and essayist, offers a chronicle of the importance of specific time alone in her *Journal of a Solitude*: "The most valuable thing we can do for the psyche, occasionally, is to let it rest, wander, live in the changing light of a room, not try to be or do anything whatever" (p. 89). She also sees solitude as being of particular service when one is feeling vulnerable because of the busyness of life with the confusion and demands it can spawn at times.

> I am here alone for the first time in weeks, to take up my "real" life again at last. That is what is strange—that friends, even passionate love, are not my real life unless there is time alone in which to explore and to discover what is happening or has happened. Without the interruptions, nourishing and maddening, this life would become arid. Yet I taste it fully only when I am alone here and "the house and I resume old conversations." . . . I often feel exhausted, but it is not my work that tires (work is a rest); it is the effort of pushing away the lives and needs of others before I can come to the work with any freshness and zest. . . . Today I feel centered and time is a friend instead of an old enemy. It was zero this morning. I have a fire burning in my study, yellow roses and mimosa on my desk. There is an atmosphere of festival, of release, in the house. We are one, the house and I, and I am happy to be alone—time to think, time to be." (pp. 11, 13, 81)

Kathleen Norris's (1993) book *Dakota: A Spiritual Geography* also treats the topic of alonetime but goes beyond it in discussing related themes like asceticism, which she refers to as "a way of surrendering to reduced circumstances in a manner that enhances the whole person" (p. 23).

Norris is not romantic about living in Dakota. She rightly recognizes that "the plains are not forgiving. Anything that is shallow—the easy optimism of a homesteader, the false hope that denies geography, climate, history; the tree whose roots don't reach ground water—will dry up and blow away" (p. 38). Yet, her appreciation of living life "in the slow lane" and the space provided when she took a step further to partake of the rhythm of a Benedictine community in North Dakota, demonstrates an honest appraisal of what the simplicity of silence and solitude has to offer—once again, not just to a writer but certainly to us as counselors as well.

> Like all who choose life in the slow lane—sailors, monks, farmers—I partake of a contemplative reality. Living close to such an expanse of land I find I have little incentive to move fast, little need of instant information. I have learned to trust the processes that take time, to value change that is not sudden or ill-considered but grows out of the ground of experience. Such change is properly defined as conversion, a word that at its roots connotes not a change of essence but of perspective, as turning round; turning back to or returning; turning one's attention to. . . . I had never before immersed myself in the kind of silence that sinks into your bones. I felt as if I were breathing deeply for the first time in years. (pp. 145, 146, 148)

Alonetime represents those periods when you are by or within yourself. Although, for most of us, silence and possibly solitude may sometimes be seen as merely gaps in our life where we are not doing something meaningful, they can be so much more when they are understood and appreciated for the experience they offer and import they can have.

Alonetime is a potential place of power. It can soften your sense of self and alter your outlook. People who know how to welcome incidental, brief, and sometimes quite prolonged periods of silence have a unique opportunity to become deeper, more generous, and open to awe. The experiences they have during these times may result in a sense of simplicity that fosters their flowing with, rather than drifting or jolting through, their lives. In the words of Admiral Richard Byrd (1938), who spent an extended time alone on a weather base in Antarctica during the winter of 1934:

> Aside from the meteorological and aural work, I had no important purposes. There was nothing of that sort. Nothing whatever except one man's desire to know that kind of experience to the full, to be by himself for a while and to taste peace and quiet and solitude long enough to find out how good they really are. . . . I wanted something more than just privacy in the geographical sense. I wanted to sink roots into some replenishing philosophy. . . . [And] I did take away something that I had not fully possessed before: appreciation of the sheer beauty and miracle of being alive, and a humble set of values. . . . Civilization has not altered my ideas. I live more simply now, and with more peace. (pp. 7, 9, 62, 63, 206)

It makes sense for counselors who deal with intense situations for much of their day, and who are not immune to serious stress in their own personal lives as well, to relish the gifts of silence and solitude. But to do this, there must be a clearer appreciation of what these gifts actually are. Otherwise, there may be questionable motivation to seek out periods of alonetime.

RECOGNIZING THE FRUITS OF BEING MINDFULLY CENTERED

Mindfulness has many benefits that can positively affect us as counselors. The following are but several, and as in the case of the reflective approach many of us employ with our clients to increase their clarity and understanding, as you read through them, if something else comes to mind, stop, savor the illustration or feeling brought forth, and let it teach its lessons. Some of the potential gifts of mindfulness are:

- Instead of anger, resentment, and other negative emotions, peace, joy, understanding, patience, and other virtues tend to become more spontaneous because we are more aware of what is going on within us at the moment.
- When someone misbehaves rather than merely reacting, we reflect and act in a helpful way just as we teach our clients to do.
- Judging ourselves or others becomes more frequently replaced by a helpful compassion that can lead to a positive change that is not possible when projection or self-blame are in place.
- We recognize more, as part of our desire to be open, that crippling guilt, which can pull us into the past and leaves us there, diminishes; we are awakened by a clear recognition of what our errors can teach us in ways that help the present and future to be different rather than pulling us back into the past and leaving us there.
- A greater appreciation of the moment we are in and the ability to move back to the present increases when we recognize that we have inordinately preoccupied ourselves with the future.

- A more natural tendency to move away from useless worry takes root in us. In its place we meet life's demands more often with a *concern* that involves: recognizing the challenges, appreciating their sources, planning what we can do, doing it, and then letting go.

- Our awareness of ourselves and those around us is more frequently marked by acceptance, compassion, and understanding.

- A deeper appreciation for patience and vulnerability instead of a desire to control becomes evident.

- Surprising episodes of gratitude for people and things we used to take for granted show themselves more readily in our daily encounters.

- There is less interest in competition and fame and instead with flowing with the unearned small joys of life (e.g., a cup of tea, a refreshing walk, children sharing their hopes, an elderly client smiling at her life).

- More experiences of collaboration and connectedness seem to spontaneously occur.

- A real sense of intrigue about our own thoughts, ways of understanding, perceptions, affect, and behavior more often replaces the old tendency toward self-blame, resentment, or fear.

- We don't automatically believe our thoughts—especially the negative ones—without checking them out.

- Self-awareness turns more into a gentle process of full self-appreciation rather than one in which we compare ourselves with others.

- We seek to be more inclusive rather than exclusive in the way we bring everything into our meditation and life.

- A desire increases in us to use our speech to benefit others by being truthful, expressive of our own experiences, sensitive to the feelings of others, supportive, encouraging, accurate, and specific rather than vague, negative, or self-referential in an exaggerated way.

Living more mindfully as described here has the ability to benefit us in many other ways as well. (See Table 3.1 and take note of them now or during a future period of alonetime.) As a matter of fact, when these positive movements in mindfulness show themselves, we can see more and more why and how facing mindlessness in the right ways allows us to be more aware during our *entire* day—not just within our meditative periods—resulting in our living more centered, full, and compassionate lives. Surely aspiring to live in such a wonderful way is a noble and rewarding goal meriting our attention, isn't it?

Table 3.1   Benefits of Movements Toward Greater Mindfulness

- Lifts us out of stagnant, obsessive thought patterns

- Alerts us to when we are not living the *experience* of life but merely wandering around in an envelope of thought thinking we are alive

- Moves us out of the thicket of preoccupations, fears, anxieties, and worries about the past or future by having us simply be where we are

- Helps us appreciate that *all* things/people/situations change

- Gives us the space to step back and get unglued from our desires, demands, and other attachments so we can have the freedom to flow with what is

- Enables us to get in touch with the invisible bonds of shame, loneliness, secrets, addictions, hopes, and other places in our heart where we have expended a great deal of energy in avoidance

- Helps us forgo the comfort of denial and avoidance for the peace that allows us to fear nothing but instead welcome all of our emotions,

Table 3.1   (Continued)

cognitions (ways of thinking, perceiving, and understanding), and impulses with compassion and clarity

- Opens up true space for others by opening it up in ourselves

- Enables us to see our defenses, failures, and growing edges as opportunities for new wisdom and openings to life (because rather than judging we are intrigued by them)

- Asks us how are we relating with ourselves—is it with kindness and clarity?

- Awakens us to our habitual, possibly deadening styles of thinking, believing, and behaving

- Allows us especially to become freer by taking "the sacred pause" suggested by spiritual guide Tara Brach when confronted with suffering. (This pause is made up of a desire to recognize what is happening, allow it, and experience it rather than trying to figure it out or control it.)

- Helps us see that permanent problems are so because of the way we formulate them, thus teaching us that loosening our grip on such ways of seeing our world makes all the difference

- Sets aside the way we have created meaning so all things can be made new

- Increases our appreciation as to how little things can produce emotional peaks and valleys in our life

- Develops our respect for both meditation and informal approaches to mindfulness that increase our awareness of "the now" during the day

- Incorporates simple practices such as taking a few moments to notice something enjoyable, appreciating our own small, beautiful acts, and slowing down when we are caught up in a sense of mindless driven action

- Encourages us to wonder more about what thoughts, emotions, and events help us create peace rather than suffering

- Teaches us that being aware is more natural when we don't seek it aggressively, or with expectations or fear that it won't produce dramatic results

(continued)

Table 3.1   (Continued)

- Has us welcome and learn from, rather than label and reject, so-called negative experiences like boredom

- Helps us be clear and to sort things out as well as deepen ourselves

- Encourages humility, helps us see our foibles, and over time increases the enjoyment we have in being with ourselves

- Results in less dependence on reinforcement by others while setting the stage for taking a healthier part in our community

- Protects our inner fire by helping us see when we need to withdraw for time alone and also uncover time within our daily activity where we can take a few breaths and center ourselves rather than be disturbed that we are being delayed or postponed in our travels or activities

Slowly reflecting on these fruits of mindfulness can help us to better notice and more fully embrace them. If you are like me, when such awareness of them is forgotten, there is a tendency to move through life like drivers arriving at their destination, having little sense of the roads they have traveled. During the stresses of life—especially when we are suffering in some way—not being spiritually mindful would be a real shame given the need we have for such awareness to continue our journey in the most alive way possible. Mindfulness awakens us so we are not as chained to unacknowledged history, early childhood experiences, and genetics. In a simple phrase: We have more freedom to be present and open to what is actually happening before and within us.

GUIDELINES FOR INNER FREEDOM

Everyone is always "unfree" in many ways. Certainly counselors are not immune to this. When we are mindful to this reality we seek to uncover and understand our resistance to change and growth in more helpful ways. So, as a way of closing this brief discussion of mindlessness, some additional guidelines for appreciating mindfulness that are worth reflecting upon at this point are offered (see Table 3.2). As in the case of other material presented in this brief book, the suggestion is that they be read slowly and reflected upon now, so relevant personal associations can rise and be savored for what they wish to teach. In addition, consideration should be given to looking at them further when expanded alonetime is made available after building such beneficial extended periods into your schedule. In reviewing them, the philosophy underlying their presentation here is that inner freedom can be enhanced by viewing illustrations in your own life that are related to the points being made in this series of guidelines.

Table 3.2   Guidelines for Inner Freedom

- Being in the now and meeting the peaceful and the painful as well as the familiar and unfamiliar leads to an acceptance of all realities and following what is good.

- Real compassion, rather than a caring that is based on guilt or duty, connects you with others in a way that fosters integration within you as well.

- Disciplines in mindfulness should include offering a gentle space to others, finding quiet honest space within yourself, and receiving guidance from others so both spaces remain free from grasping and the desire for gain.

- Facing your fears, doubts, boredom, anxieties, anger, charlatanism, and manipulative nature doesn't require much courage when you have humility.

- Meditation is made up of a little technique and a lot of gentle love.

- Sadness may come in the silence because that is when this hidden teacher may feel welcome to show her helpful face as a reminder that you may be holding onto something less than the truth.

(*continued*)

Table 3.2 (Continued)

- Once you let the pain of an interpersonal encounter wash over and away from you, what is left is a clean truth about yourself that a less relaxed encounter could not produce in a million years.

- Acknowledging easily and openly both what you're praised and condemned for, then where there was once negative passion will be new wisdom and the continued freedom only humility can bring.

- Strong emotions are always the smoke of the fire of attachment.

- Seeing both a beautiful sunny morning and a relaxing rainy afternoon as reminders that love is around you and that the hurt, doubt, and resentment you may have are little parts of your life that need to be released.

- Life is no longer small and unrewarding when you get excited about how you can grow spiritually and be naturally compassionate.

- Flowing with life doesn't stop the pain; nothing can do that. Yet it does lessen unnecessary suffering, teach new lessons, and help one to see the value of having patience for new openings. As Thomas Merton says: "Courage comes and goes; hold on for the next supply."(Source unknown)

- Mindfulness is not designed to make you special. True ordinariness is tangible wonder.

- Every period in your life brings new gifts. If you use old techniques and attitudes fail to change, you won't be able to open those gifts.

- Persons who really love inner freedom demonstrate it by being open to seeing specific truths about themselves without resentment, hostility, or fear.

- Being able to enjoy life as it is given takes practice, whereas thinking wistfully about life is easy.

- Mindful persons enjoy life's daily wealth while those around them dream of silly things like wealth, fame, power, and others finding them attractive.

- Those who respect everyone have a wealth of spiritual teachers.

Table 3.2   (Continued)

- Psychologist and Eastern spiritual writer Anthony de Mello (1986) used to tell people, "It is easier to put on slippers than to carpet the whole of the earth" (p. 88). Perspective that comes with being mindful prevents you from entering "the carpeting business."

- Embarrassment, failure, and awkwardness are handles of new knowledge.

- What people call "happiness" is often really a passing high, after which they will have a corresponding low.

- One of the greatest gifts you can give to yourself is to observe yourself with interest but not judgment.

- Being mindful, open, and free often requires that you forgo pleasing both living and dead family members and friends.

- Take from every positive role model something to practice in life.

- While you need to be open to all people, you must develop and nurture a circle of friends who will challenge, support, nurture, and inspire you (as well as make you laugh when you need to!).

- If you wish to be free in spirit only for yourself, then you have failed already; if you wish to be free for others too, then your compassionate purpose will purify you.

Still, knowing all of this and actually practicing and experiencing it is obviously a very different story. Consequently, to look at our own level of mindfulness is also a process in which we learn further the art of leaning back as well as appreciating our own resistance to daily awareness or spending time in silence and solitude. An awareness of such potential blocks can make all the difference, especially if we conduct that search with a balance of clarity and kindness for ourselves.

Questions to Consider at This Point

Several tables were provided in this chapter so that reflecting on aspects of mindfulness would encourage seeing its value and lead to informal and formal practices on improving and relishing awareness. To help in this regard, and by way of closing this chapter, the following questions are provided to stir up discussions within yourself and possibly a mentor on what may be contributing to avoiding or not taking full advantage of being nonjudgmentally in the now. They are presented in the form of an Awareness Questionnaire.

AWARENESS QUESTIONNAIRE

Are you easily distracted?

Do you find yourself reflecting on the past a good deal and replaying it in your head as if you could change the outcome, even though in your heart you know you can't?

How often during the day are you preoccupied with the future?

Do you find yourself driving, walking, or going through your daily routine on automatic pilot?

If your positive predictions for the day don't come true, does it spoil the event or interaction for you?

Do you stay in your head for much of the day and not enjoy the sensations and experiences you encounter?

Do you avoid looking directly at the realities in your life?

How you look physically?

> The pains and losses in your life?
>
> Your own mortality?
>
> The world's need for compassion and your ways of responding to this need?

Do you continue to use approaches that you know in your heart no longer make sense?

Do you realize that if you let go of certain habits, styles, and gratifications, you can be happier but still go down the same psychological roads?

Do you build your image of happiness on the "If only ____ happened, then life would be great" theory?

Are you mentally with your clients, family, and friends, or is your mind elsewhere in most instances?

Are certain "flowers" in your garden of experiences in life so precious that you are ignoring the others?

Do you find yourself recognizing that there are life joys to experience but you can't seem to let go of what's holding you back in enjoying them?

Do you spend more time planning and striving than actually enjoying life?

Are you aware of the elements of your life that remain unlived and untapped and have a plan to address them immediately? (One of the worst enemies of mindfulness is to believe you still have time, which allows you to postpone your life for "practical" reasons.)

CHAPTER

4

Learning the Art of Leaning Back

Leaning back from the pressures of being a counselor can open the gates to lanes of greater inner freedom not yet traveled. Yet, today most of us leave those portals unopened. We may not even know they are there or think they are only discoverable by something akin to magic, luck, fame, or winning a major psychological or spiritual lottery (i.e., finding the "perfect" relationship, position, or financial arrangement for our work and *then* we will be free). But as enticing as these images are advertised to be in our culture or mind, entertaining them on a continual basis only leads us into emotional and intellectual dead ends, whereas stepping back in the right way, possibly during periods of alonetime, can provide us with the leads and space we need—not only for ourselves but also for those we counsel.

Silence, solitude, and mindful moments have the power to stop us in our tracks and ask, Why are we continuing to live this way?—a very possibly disconcerting question to a counselor who is in the business of guiding others to often answer this existential query. And, when we say, "We *must* live this way. We have no choice. It is practical and normal so there is really no other way." Paradoxically, the first gate to new freedom opens to some degree because in our hearts, in saying this, we already know at some level that what we are telling ourselves is not true. Once this initial portal of reality that can give us space to gain a healthier, freer perspective is nudged open a bit, it may still be ignored or temporarily forgotten by us, but it will never close completely again—and that is what the permanent gift of leaning back for the first time offers us.

Yet, silence and solitude—the places into which we can take a breath—are surprisingly not in favor anymore. As we have noted, they may even be suspect. Thoreau recognized this many years ago and wrote,

> If a man walks in the woods for love of them half of each day, he is in danger as being regarded as a loafer. But if he spends his days as a spectator, shearing off those woods and making the earth bald before her time, he is deemed an industrious and enterprising citizen. (Source unknown)

Such Thoreau-styled protests, thank goodness, are starting to become more frequent. People are increasingly recognizing that even relationships, as good and essential as they are, rely on our having time alone. As psychologist and spiritual writer Henri Nouwen (1981) points out,

> We have been made to believe that feelings, emotions, and even the inner stirrings of our soul have to be shared with others. Expressions such as "Thanks for sharing this with me," or "It was good to share this with you." show that the door of our steambath is open most of the time. In fact, people who prefer to keep to themselves and do not expose their interior life tend to create uneasiness and are often considered inhibited, asocial,

or simply odd. But let us at least raise the question of whether our lavish ways of sharing are not more compulsive than virtuous; that instead of creating community they tend to flatten out our life together. Often we come home from a sharing session with a feeling that something precious has been taken away from us. (p. 53)

He then goes on to note,

It is in solitude that this compassionate solidarity grows. In solitude we realize that nothing human is alien to us, that the roots of all conflict, war, injustice, cruelty, hatred, jealousy, and envy are deeply anchored in our own heart. In solitude our heart of stone can be turned into a heart of flesh, a rebellious heart into a contrite heart, and a closed heart into a heart that can open itself to all suffering people in a gesture of solidarity. (p. 34)

THE CAPACITY TO BE ALONE: RECOGNIZING WE ARE NOT USED TO SILENCE, MUCH LESS SOLITUDE

Once I was leading a couple of days of retreat and restoration at the New Jersey shore for Methodist ministers. On the first day I suggested—a bit timidly since they were professional persons of prayer—that they take at least two minutes in silence and solitude and wrapped in gratitude each morning to center themselves before they began their intense day of service to others. In mentioning only two minutes, my goal was to encourage regularity—*Anyone can do two minutes*, I thought—and to circumvent the usual resistance I experience when suggesting periods of alonetime (i.e., "I just don't have time in my busy schedule").

The next morning one of the ministers in the queue for breakfast asked if she might sit with me. "Of course," I said, and we completed gathering what we wished to eat and sat down together. I smiled at her and asked if she would like to say Grace before the meal, which she did. We then ate slowly, and finally there was a period over coffee when she shared the question she had. She asked, "Do you really take those two minutes each morning that you suggested to us yesterday?" When I said I really did, she paused and said, "I did it this morning. Two minutes seemed like a long time!" and we both had to laugh.

Surprisingly, short periods of silence and solitude may not be easy for us—even when we seem to be in the mindfulness or prayerfulness business. People who take alonetime seriously know this. In one of his diaries, Thomas Merton (1988) offered the following question and hope that demonstrates the respect all of us should have when we approach quiet time alone. He wrote, "Solitude is a stern master who brooks no nonsense. And the question arises—am I so full of nonsense that she will cast me out? I pray she will not" (p. 154).

Knowing how to be alone is, for the most part, a truly unhonored art that requires both guidance and discipline. Failing to appreciate this fact can result in self-absorption or moodiness, on the one hand, or a contamination of solitude with an unnecessary myriad of activities or noise on the other. Mere silence and solitude need not lead to greater perspective and gratitude. It can lead elsewhere, as was reported by a spiritual leader of persons who had ostensibly dedicated their whole lives to finding spiritual wisdom and being compassionate, in the following words:

> Someone said to me that these older persons of ministry keep replaying their lives over and over hoping that the ending will be different—and, of course, it never is.

I have heard stories of people who make the break-through to forgiveness and die soon after and find the peace that sets us free. However, such persons in certain groups—even though they have spent lifetimes in being compassionate—are often rarer than I'd like to say.

THE PSYCHOLOGICAL CAPACITY TO BE ALONE

As was previously noted, psychiatrist Anthony Storr (1988), in his seminal work *Solitude: A Return to the Self*, opened up a discussion among psychotherapists concerning the value of alonetime. He cited the work of Winnicott to make his case on the importance of the capacity to be alone. One of the more intriguing points he made as a part of his argument is the following one:

Winnicott suggests that the capacity to be alone in adult life originates with the infant's experience of being *alone in the presence of the mother*. He is postulating a state in which the infant's immediate needs, for food, warmth, physical contact and so on, have been satisfied, so that there is no need for the infant to be looking to the mother for anything, nor any need for her to be concerned with anything. . . . I find his conceptions illuminating. He is suggesting that the capacity to be alone originally, depends upon what Bowlby would call secure attachment: that is, upon the child being able peacefully to be itself in the presence of the mother without anxiety about her possible departure, and without anxiety as to what may or may not be expected by her. . . .

But Winnicott goes further. He suggests that the capacity to be alone, first in the presence of the mother, and then in her absence, is also related to the individual's capacity to get in touch with, and make manifest, his own true inner feelings. It is only when the child has experienced a contented, relaxed sense of being alone with, and then without, the mother, that he can be sure of being able to discover what he really needs or wants, irrespective of what others may expect or try to foist upon him.

The capacity to be alone thus becomes linked with self-discovery and self-realization; with becoming aware of one's deepest needs, feelings, and impulses. (pp. 20–21)

Storr then goes on to also make a connection to Winnicott's concept regarding the capacity to be alone with the value of meditation. He notes that this version of alonetime facilitates a person's ability to integrate previously unconnected thoughts and feelings by allowing him or her the time and space to accomplish this valuable objective. He goes on to point out that from his vantage point that:

Being able to get in touch with one's deepest thoughts and feelings, and providing time for them to regroup themselves into new formations and combinations, are important aspects of the creative process, as well as a way of relieving tension and promoting mental health.

It appears, therefore, that some development of the capacity to be alone is necessary if the brain is to function at its best, and if the individual is to fulfill his highest potential. Human beings easily become alienated from their own deepest needs and feelings. Learning, thinking, innovation, and maintaining contact with one's own inner world are all facilitated by solitude. (p. 28)

WHAT ACTUALLY IS TRUE AWARENESS AND MINDFULNESS?

Still, given what Storr and others say about the value of alone-time, silence and solitude do not produce value in and of themselves. A sense of mindfulness, which essentially is quite simple (but not easy) must be repeatedly relearned as adults no matter how committed we say we are to being aware and appreciative of what is before us. On the other hand, mindfulness is actually a state that young children often appreciate naturally, almost without effort. Jerry Braza (1997), in his book *Moment by Moment*, reflects upon his daughter's awe of the now:

I recall a time driving my young children somewhere when we approached a railroad crossing as the lights began to flash and the safety gate went down. My first thought was "Oh no! We're going to be held up by a train and be late." Just then, my daughter called out from the backseat, "Daddy, Daddy, we're so lucky! We get to watch the train go by!" Her awareness of the present moment was a wonderful reminder to stop and enjoy what the journey had to offer along the way. (p. 3)

In this story (taken from a book on the art and practice of mindfulness), we can see the importance of paying attention to where you are and what you are doing. Often "the now" is filled with many gifts if we have the eyes to see them, and this can be learned by knowing the basics of mindfulness. When the counselor does know this information, it has dual use with both clients and possibly even more powerfully with him- or herself.

As Germer (2005) reports and suggests in one of the essays in the edited work *Mindfulness and Psychotherapy,*

> Any exercise that alerts us to the present moment, with acceptance, cultivates mindfulness. . . . Examples are directing attention to one's breathing, listening to ambient sounds in the environment, paying attention to our posture at a given moment, labeling feelings, and so forth. The list is endless. . . . Two common exercises for cultivating mindfulness in daily life . . . involve slowly walking and slow eating. (p. 14).

PAYING ATTENTION DIFFERENTLY IN SOLITUDE

Being alone for some people may mean many different things. For some it may be a chance to do mindless activity. For others, though, whether they are straightening a closet or planting a row of tulips, the activity or time sitting quietly is spent mindfully. Obviously then, the difference in approach is significant, not only in how we understand it but also in the results that occur as well as how we greet them.

Mindfulness allows life to come up before the person without judgment during periods of silence and possibly solitude. (Sounds a bit like the counseling process in its ideal, doesn't it?) It has the person leaving nothing out, while not indulging anything either negatively or positively. In a spirit of mindfulness, the person experiences and learns. The process simply involves watching, breathing, and living in the now—ideally with a sense of wonder. But it doesn't seem so simple, and writers and guides on mindfulness offer guidance to keep the process as elementary as an unvarnished stone. Included in such guidance is that with mindfulness:

- Everything is fresh each time: Expectations—even if they are based on history of how something originally happened in the past—defeat this.
- Awareness of even mindlessness doesn't lead to regret that we are not in the present but "merely" encourages us to return to the now when we get trapped in the past or pre-occupied with the future.
- Includes not the ideal but the real rather than positive or negative fantasies or concepts.
- An appreciation is held deeply that everything, *every* thing changes.
- Encourages counselors to see—honestly and completely—how every action and comment has an affect on the client—and to some degree on themselves.
- Appreciates not general philosophies as much as specific effects of the words and actions taken.

The sense of *awareness* (or what most refer to as mindfulness) that we value as counselors and the openness we truly embrace can make the difference in how we value a life of truth, presence, and being awake and in turn how it makes itself known in our clinical practice and life.

Mindfulness ensures that we are awake. It also sets the stage for important learning during the difficult times in our life "if only we have the eyes to see." On the other hand, mindlessness not only keeps us blind to all that we should be grateful for but also prevents us from being all that we can truly be—no matter what is going on in our life at any given time. As part of our journey to become more awake, we must be able to pick up and attend to the unique characteristics of mindfulness. Some of them include:

- A clear awareness of what you are experiencing, thinking, or feeling without judging yourself or others
- A sense of intrigue about yourself and others without projection (blaming others), self-condemnation, discouragement, or expectations
- More interest in discovering the gifts of life rather than merely focusing on your accomplishments
- An appreciation of being in the now and a willingness to return to the present when you are drawn into the past or begin to be preoccupied by the future
- A spirit of "unlearning" and a willingness to see life differently that is inspired by the call to "make all things new"
- A non-ego-centered approach to life that recognizes that it isn't all about *me*
- A willingness to recognize, embrace, and flow with change
- A spirit of receiving life as it is without reaction or rejection
- A focus on those activities that create well-being instead of suffering for others—and *ourselves*
- Appreciation of the beauty of patience and enjoying the process of life rather than solely looking forward to completions or successes
- An interest in letting go of the training we have received in grasping, being envious, angry, and unkind and instead an openness to sharing without an expectation of getting anything in return, being intrigued by our responses so we can learn from them rather than responding by being defensive or self-indicting, and slowing down rather than straining toward goals (even perceived good ones)

- Avoidance of comparing ourselves favorably or unfavorably with others
- A greater desire to be sensitive to how our words and actions affect others
- An interest in seeking—even in little ways—to contribute to well-being rather than suffering for others and ourselves
- Openness to "mindfully touching" all of our denials, loneliness, shame, and negative feelings about ourselves with compassion rather than running away from them
- Allowing information, negative and positive, familiar and unfamiliar, to flow to us without being obstructed or modified by our ego or fears
- An increased desire for transparency and being persons without guile in the way we live so we can help purify—rather than contaminate with our defensiveness—the spiritual atmosphere in which we and others live

Practicing, not just knowing about, these characteristics of mindfulness results in being open to receive all that life might offer. In addition, and of possibly even more importance, doing this will help you face life's difficulties, gray periods, or sad experiences and deepen you in ways you may never have dreamed possible, which will be a gift to those you counsel. In the case of extreme stress or trauma, the literature on *posttraumatic growth* points to this reality (Werdel & Wicks, 2012).

RELEASING PREVIOUSLY UNACCOUNTED-FOR ENERGY

As counselors we spend much of the day in front of a mirror whose distortions are dramatic because of the positive and negative transferences attributed to us by the people we treat, supervise, mentor, and teach (as well as, unfortunately at times, by some of the colleagues with whom we work). These distortions from the outside also trigger in some cases our own longstanding (characterological) inner and situational blind spots. Fortunately, meditation and mindful awareness can wash these up to the surface of our consciousness (especially when we have a gentle, clear mentor with whom to process). When this happens, all we need do is not close our eyes. Yet, psychologically, often without knowing it, we at the very least "squint."

Jack Kornfield (1993), recognizing this tendency, recalls the guidance of his teacher, Achaan Chah, who said that in meditation, metaphorically,

> Just go into the room and put one chair in the center. Take the one seat in the center of the room, open the doors and windows, and see who comes to visit. You will witness all kinds of scenes and actors, all kinds of temptations and stories, everything imaginable. Your only job is to stay in your seat. You will see it all arise and pass, and out of this, wisdom and understanding will come. (p. 31)

In doing this, Kornfield suggests we are creating space in ourselves that allows memories and emotions to rise and teach us where our unaccounted-for energy that is hidden in unrecognized sadness and shame, resentment and regret, desire and loneliness, and even happiness and joy, lies.

Knowing this is important not just for us but also for those we interact with and influence—for good or for bad. Many people come to us as psychological exiles from their former lives. Who they thought they were or their world was no longer makes sense to them, especially after experiencing trauma, serious stress, or significant loss.

In a way, once they have encountered such an onslaught on themselves and their world of meaning, as the literature on post-traumatic growth (PTG) teaches us, they are free to pursue the future without old limitations. However, if we as their counselors are still operating out of an outmoded structure ourselves, it is difficult or impossible for us to help them take advantage of the possibilities that might come to the fore for them. Instead, we may see posttraumatic stress gains not heretofore possible had the unwanted event not happened or remained as mere delusion or denial on the client's part.

CREATING FAMILIAR PLACES OF SOLITUDE

One of the most practical steps that can be taken to include mindfulness meditation as a part of our daily life is to have familiar places in which to experience it. Yet, such places in the world seem so limited today that we must take extra steps to discover them. In Sara Maitland's (2008) words:

> Silence, even as an expression of awe, is becoming uncomfortable. We are asked to be silent less and less; churches and public libraries are no longer regarded as places where silence is appropriate . . . silence is not experienced as refreshing or as assisting concentration, but as threatening and disturbing. . . . Nonetheless, despite the rising tide of noise, there are some real pools of silence embedded in the noisiest places and I began to search them out. (pp. 37–38)

She reflects further in *A Book of Silence* on how important silence and solitude is for a writer. She also shares that when she moved to a house away from everything how a friend of hers reacted, which I think tells us once again something about much of society's view of alonetime today, yet how persons who love their space, that is their physical and spiritual environment, differ in their perception of it.

Virginia Woolf famously taught us that every woman writer needs a room of her own. She didn't know the half of it, in my opinion. I need a moor of my own. Or, as an exasperated but obviously sensitive friend commented when she came to see my latest lunacy, "Only you, Sara— twenty mile views of absolutely nothing!"

It isn't "nothing," actually—it is cloud formations, and the different ways reed, rough grass, heather and bracken move in the wind, and the changing colours, not just through the year but through the day as the sun and the clouds alternate and shift . . . and it is the huge nothing that pulls me into itself. I looked at it, and with fewer things to look at I see better. . . . I can see occasional, and apparently unrelated, strips of silver, which are in fact the small river meandering down the valley. . . . I think about how beautiful it is, and how happy I am. (pp. 1–3)

Thoreau, one of the leading contemporary muses for the need for silence and solitude, felt he could not preserve his health and spirits if he did not spend a significant time sauntering "through the woods and over the hills and fields absolutely free from worldly engagements." We may not have as much time as Thoreau did to devote to such endeavors. In addition, we may not wish to find ourselves in a rural setting. As a matter of fact, sometimes we may think of solitude as a back-to-nature movement such as Thoreau, and later Maitland, seemed to be suggesting. However, this needn't be the case.

Hugh Prather, for instance, notes that

> what is conducive to concentration for one person is not for another. Solitude is often associated with the fact of getting away from people, and into nature, but my wife Gayle, for example, is more at rest in a large city than in the wilderness. "Nature makes you itch," she says. She's convinced that camping out invites angry bears and ax murderers. And certainly it makes no sense to say that in order to feel what connects us all, we must always get away from each other. (Salwak, 1998, p. 11)

However, with an appreciation of mindful silence, our time—however long or wherever it may be—can still have a significant influence on us for the better. The goal is not to run away but to find those spaces that are conducive to us.

With respect to time and space, George Prochnik (2010), in his recent popular work, *In Pursuit of Silence: Listening for Meaning in a World of Noise*, notes that

> We probably do not need a pervasive silence—desirable as this might seem to some. What we do need is more space in which we can interrupt our general experience of noise. What we must aspire to is a greater proportion of quiet in the course of everyday life. (p. 283)

He then goes on to point out a reality about taking significant periods of silence that is worth reflecting on so it doesn't become a source of resistance to taking any time at all:

> I cherish the memory of the time I spent on a silent retreat at an ashram, gazing at a group of people scattered across a grassing hillside like roosting birds—all of them concentrated on doing nothing but being still and listening to the natural world. But the people who go to ashrams, vipassana centers, and all the rich variants of silent-meditation retreats are, for the most part, reasonably well off. Like me, they had the money, the time, or simply the social context that enabled them to wake up one day and say to themselves, "You know what? I'm going on a silent retreat." I'm worried about all the people who, for one reason or another, lack the resources to discover what silence can bring. (p. 288)

Still, all of us can access quiet places if we have the eyes to see them, so we should keep this in mind. They include places of worship in our large cities that are open during the day, possibly between services. Libraries, small urban gardens or large parks, walkways along rivers and streams, and little coffeehouses during the off hours are but a few such places that quickly come to mind. We need to be aware of what could double as a place of refuge instead of simply dismissing the possibilities as a way of saying, "I can't do it. There is no place available for me."

We also need to take the energy to make a conducive place for ourselves in our homes and offices so that when the opportunity spontaneously presents itself or we have initiated a ritual of silence during our day (i.e., morning meditation or quiet reflection), then we know where we will do it.

For some, it may be a corner of a room or a separate place. It need not be fancy, just enhancing to the process of silence and solitude. Jesuit priest and author of works on spirituality, Richard Hauser, writes:

> I [meditate] in my own room—which doubles as a bedroom—in a chair next to a large window with an eastward exposure, overlooking the secluded garden mentioned earlier; the chair faces my prayer wall. It is upholstered and comfortable, but supports me firmly in an upright position. Alongside the chair on a side table I place all the materials I need. . . . I love this room; it is away from my offices. The window, open in warm weather, gives direct access to the sights and sounds of the garden and to the warmth and light of the rising sun. My prayer wall is hung with favorite icons, prints, and crucifixes gathered over the years; I rearrange the wall for different liturgical seasons and feasts. The physical setting—the time, place, furniture arrangement—is key. . . . [Meditation] can be simple: Just find the right time and place and go there regularly! (Hauser, 2000, p. 387)

SIMPLE APPROACHES TO FORMAL MINDFULNESS MEDITATION

Once we have addressed the issue of where (conducive places), the question of how comes to mind. As well as improving our sense of nonjudgmental mindfulness/awareness in general, we also need to simultaneously attend to our formal meditation practice if we wish to have one. To help readers who are not familiar with meditation practice, the following simple suggestions are offered to foster a beginning practice. (Further reading from selections in the recommended books on the topic listed in the bibliography at the end of this book, plus the use of a mentor or guide, if you wish one, will help develop and deepen your practice.)

- *Have a conducive posture.* As we sit, with our back straight, we look just ahead of us at something that can hold our attention (e.g., a candle) as we breathe naturally and gently.
- *Be patient.* Rushing or expecting something only injects unnecessary pressure into our time of meditation. Be the apple slowly ripening.
- *Don't unduly entertain, judge, or run away from your thoughts.* Just observe and let them move through you like water in a slowly running stream. To help accomplish this, you can label thoughts ("judging," "guilt") that come your way, use a centering word/mantra like "gentle," or even count your breaths one to four and keep counting this way until you are present again.
- *Accept where you are in meditation and don't compare.* After all, what choice do you have other than to be where you are at this point? Also, don't waste time in favorably or unfavorably comparing your meditation, or anything about yourself, with others. Meditation is not a competition.
- *Don't seek to solve anything in meditation.* Problem solving is a good activity, but it is not appropriate to formal mindfulness.
- *Don't expect or try to force anything.* Just relax; that's enough. Trust. The meditation will do the rest. There will be times when we are meditating that it will flow easily. Other times our meditation may seem flat empty. We may

even be bored for a time. That's all right. As Zen teaches us: If you are bored for two minutes in meditation, then do it for four!

- *Don't cling.* Just breathe in good energy and breathe out peace, then let whatever comes up flow through you like a light wind. If some issue or theme repeatedly comes up, just come back to your centering word or counting your breaths by counting from one to four again and again until you are settled. Remember that letting your meditation move with your breathing in and out is an anchor in meditation.

- *Although you should be regular in meditation, allow for times of intense, longer meditative periods.* Taking at least a few moments each day to center yourself is essential. Being disciplined to pray regularly is the spiritual backbone of a life well-lived. However, if possible, there should be times when you extend your prayer for longer periods of time. (Wicks, 2010)

INCLUDING EVERYTHING

One of the most important elements of mindfulness meditation is to include everything in one's practice. Jack Kornfield (1995), in his Eastern spirituality work, *A Path with Heart*, notes:

I had hoped for special effects from meditation—happiness, special states of rapture, extraordinary experiences. But that was not primarily what my teacher offered. He offered a way of life, a lifelong path of awakening, attention, surrender, and commitment. He offered a happiness that was not dependent on any of the changing conditions of the world but came out of one's own difficult and conscious inner transformation. In join-ing the monastery, I had hoped to leave behind the pain of my family life and the difficulties of the world, but of course they followed me. It took many years for me to realize that these difficulties were part of my practice. . . . The simple phrase, "This too, this too," was the main meditation instruction of [another of the spiritual mas-ters] with whom I studied. Through these few words we were encouraged to soften and open to see whatever we encountered, accepting the truth with a wise and under-standing heart. (p. 5)

What makes mindfulness rich is including all of the specifics of life. When something joyful, puzzling, sad, or upsetting hap-pens—no matter how little it seems at first—remembering to say "this too, this too" must be brought to your meditation and mind-fulness. Seeing even what you feel are distractions as sources for new knowledge is a response that will reap great rewards. The goal of this approach is to transform all of your life into a mindful life. In this way, rather than being tied down by so many other "voices" (culture, peer pressure, family fears, neediness—even the profes-sional counseling field) in your life, you can respond to the truth's sometimes soft inner voice that is calling you to new freedom and living more fully.

GOING ON RETREAT: PERIODS OF DRAMATIC SOLITUDE

Philosopher Henri Thoreau (1853) is probably one of the best-known Americans who sought after significant periods of soli-tude. Much like Admiral Byrd's earlier comments on what he was seeking, Thoreau's description as to why he did this remains compelling today:

> I went to the woods because I wished to live deliberately, to front only the essential facts of life, and see if I could not learn what it had to teach, and not, when I came to die, discover that I had not lived. I did not wish to live what was not life, living is so dear; nor did I wish to practice resignation, unless it was quite necessary. I wanted to live deep and suck out all the marrow of life, to live so sturdily and Spartan-like as to put to rout all that was not life, to cut a broad swath and shave close, to drive life into a corner, and reduce it to its lowest terms, and, if it proved to be mean, why then to get the whole and genuine meanness of it, and publish its meanness to the world; or if it were sublime, to know it by experience, and be able to give a true account of it in my next excursion.

More dramatic than Thoreau's retreat to the woods is the one described in *A Woman in the Polar Night* by Christiane Ritter (1954/2010). In the Introduction, Lawrence Millman writes:

> Stuck in the hut by herself during an epic snowstorm, Christiane almost did go crazy. At the same time, she realized that, however tough the circumstances, she could survive them. And from then on, she did not think of the Arctic as an enemy. Rather, it was a realm "where everything goes its prescribed way . . . without man's intervention." Such was her transformation that she could even suggest that "in centuries to come, men will go to the Arctic as in biblical times they withdrew to the desert, to

find the truth again." I can't imagine any polar explorer making a statement like this. . . .

Christiane left what she called "the Arctic wilderness" in June of 1935, never to return . . . she didn't really need to return . . . since she brought it home with her, or at least brought home a radically different way of looking at the world. A short while after she got back from Spitsbergen, the Ritter family estate burned to the ground. But rather than go into mourning over the loss of her home and virtually all of her possessions, Christiane was more or less grateful, according to her daughter Karin. For she could now live simply, without a surfeit of ballast, just as she lived in the hut in Grahuken. (pp. 5–6)

Her own reactions to living in a very small hut alone for protracted periods of time are interesting to read. A flavor of the lessons she learned come through well in her published memoir on the experiences she had. They are filled with the gratitude that can only come after deprivation when one feels new appreciation of what is often taken for granted.

Much less dramatic than these accounts though are the reflections of people who go on a silent retreat by themselves or with others who will also respect the need to move away from noise and even good conversation for awhile. Such a period may be for 30 days, a week, or as is a more likely scenario for those of us in the counseling field, an overnight or weekend experience. From such a time taken, the many helpers I have interviewed report a combination of—in their own interpretation—pleasant and disagreeable experiences such as:

- Recognizing how much was swirling around in my mind just below the surface

- How I had forgotten what the simple truth really is because even conversations within myself often sounded like cocktail party discussions
- I realized I rarely challenged my shame but covered it over with intellectualizations (i.e., "I crossed those boundaries with that client because she needed extra physical assurance of my interest in her").
- There were fears in me that if I saw how I needed to change and did it, others would shy away from me, I would see how I had not really lived up to this point in my life, or if I did see the truth I would have to do something about it.

Despite such descriptions of the experiences encountered in silence and possibly solitude, in the end, most of what persons who retreated from society felt, thought, and experienced eventually seemed to turn out to be informative, and thus beneficial, to them in ways that would not have been possible had they not taken a longer period of solitude. Most of us only avail ourselves of a few hours or possibly even a day.

Alonetime, like anger and most other encounters or reactions, are not beneficial in and of themselves. It is our approach to, and perception of, them that makes all the difference. That is why the information on informal and formal mindfulness (meditation) that helps us to lean back from both our busy schedules and minds filled with thoughts and judgments is so necessary. It is also essential to recognize the natural resistances we have to spending time alone so we can continue to enhance our alonetime rather than succumb to our blocks to it. To conclude here, in the words of the poet Rilke (1934/1993):

[F]or what (ask yourself) would solitude be that had no greatness; there is but *one* solitude, and that is great, and not easy to bear, and to almost everybody come hours when they would gladly exchange it for any sort of intercourse, however banal and cheap, for the semblance of some slight accord with the first comer, with the unworthiest. . . . But perhaps those are the very hours when solitude grows. . . . But that must not mislead you. The necessary thing is after all but this: solitude, great inner solitude. Going-into-oneself and for hours meeting no one—this one must be able to attain. To be solitary, the way one was solitary as a child, when the grownups went around involved with things that seemed important and big because they themselves looked so busy and because one comprehended nothing of their doings. . . . And you should not let yourself be confused in your solitude by the fact that there is something in you that wants to break out of it. This very wish will help you, if you use it quietly, and deliberately and like a tool, to spread out your solitude over wide country. (pp. 45, 46, 53)

☞ Some Questions to Consider at This Point

In your own life, how would you describe the relationship between alonetime and the relationships you have as a counselor and within your personal life?

What has been your own array of experiences when you took time in silence and possibly solitude?

If you have a formal mindfulness meditative practice, how do you handle distractions during meditation?

What unique characteristics of mindfulness have you experienced and which ones noted in this chapter have you not? How do you understand this pattern?

What are you favorite places of solitude?

What are the most important approaches to meditation for you?

If you use a diary to note your reflections after meditation or periods of alonetime, in what ways has this practice been helpful for you?

If you don't record your impressions, do you think you might begin? What would it take for you to do this?

CHAPTER
5

Experiencing a New Type of Counselor Self-Nurturance

During the Afghanistan and Iraqi wars, I was invited to speak to military chaplains and their assistants in Germany. As I stood apart from the group for a moment during the break, one of the senior chaplains approached me. Then, as he surveyed the room with sadness in his eyes, he said in a low voice to me, "There are a lot of ghosts here. There is nothing left inside them."

Caregivers are in a privileged position: to help those suffering physical illness, psychological anxiety, stress, depression, and spiritual crises. Yet, very honorable roles come at a price and come with a caution: If you don't take care of yourself, you too may fall victim to the problems in others that you may be trying to alleviate.

Even when those problems don't represent spikes in client stress, the discipline of being in a counseling role can become disturbing to our sense of inner balance. As Storr (1988) notes, "If society is to function smoothly, there are bound to be occasions when one has to present; be welcoming when one is tired; smile when one wants to groan; or in other ways put on an act.

Such dissimulation can be fatiguing" (p. 94). In counseling, this experience is even more frequent and intensive.

Counseling is also one of those professions that doesn't cease at the end of the day. This doesn't mean that counselors should take their work home with them or that they should constantly be involved in the business of diagnosis and providing prescriptions for new behaviors for their family and co-workers. (I have a sense that our family, friends, and associates might not appreciate this.) What I am suggesting though is that the *spirit* of one's counseling should reflect the character of one's entire life. Yet, this is not practical if one is not kind and attentive to oneself.

When persons become counselors, they have finished a training program but have only begun the journey to fully appreciate compassion. Psychologist and Zen Master Jack Kornfield (2000) illustrates appreciating this reality in his own life.

> I had finished my Ph.D. in psychology and I found myself working in an adolescent unit and in suicide prevention. For years I had believed psychology had all the answers I was looking for. But as I worked, my faith began to crack. Because of the vast unalleviated suffering I encountered, the idea that psychology could give me all the answers seemed ridiculous. What could I turn to understand this life?
>
> One day in 1972 I visited a friend in Berkeley and as we walked she encountered a jolly bright foreign man and began a conversation with him. Later she explained he was a Tibetan lama and invited me to his teachings on dreams. I didn't understand a word of it, but at one moment when a woman questioned him about

compassionate action, and I saw the way he answered, compassion was no longer just a word. He brought into his answer a manifestation of compassion that totally touched my heart. I was stunned. Up until that time I had thought of compassion as a nice Presbyterian word that had no reality; you know a nice idea. Here was a living force. I was completely intrigued. I wanted to know what this was. That opened the spiritual door for me. (p. 12)

What we lack in our appreciation of the true meaning of being a compassionate presence may whisper to us before we become a caregiver. After we enter the profession, the whisper often turns into a scream as we face the intense interpersonal challenges of those we treat. (Unless of course we simply defend ourselves by uselessly "yelling back" through the use of intellectualization, overconcern with financial recompense, etc.)

This deeper recognition of compassion then asks us several larger questions, which if faced, can bring us deeper as we seek to be more genuinely present to others:

- How can facing our disappointments and dissatisfaction as counselors, with clients, colleagues and supervisors, or the profession in general paradoxically lead to greater fulfillment—not only as professionally but personally as well?
- What called us to be counselors initially, and what calls us to be counselors now?
- While we seek to be a compassionate presence to others, in what ways might we feel starved of compassion ourselves?

- How are we encountering the active life most of us as counselors live, and what are the ways we are simply ignoring what we would encourage others to enjoy?
- What is our style of addressing conflict? How is this style working, and what needs to change?
- How are we enjoying our life *now* rather than delaying gratification in ways that are not a sign of maturity but actually evidence of denial of one's death and a failure to be mindful and appreciative of one's own life?
- What is the source of meaning-making in one's own life so being a counselor is only a technical task?
- What are the dreams, shame, resentments, desires, ideas, and loves we avoid? (This may be glimpsed during a state of "diminished consciousness"—dreams, when fatigued, under the influence of alcohol, medication, or drugs, after a period of extreme stress or a rejection/disagreement.)

To face these questions doesn't mean taking a journey in self-confrontation (although at certain junctures it may feel or be that way). It actually can only be done with a willingness on the part of counselors to touch everything within themselves with compassion. This then raises the question: What does true compassion for counselors involve?

COUNSELOR SELF-NURTURANCE

The answer to this question isn't what most people think unless they have a true interest in the inner life. Often it is confused with self-care (which is important, and I have sought to address in *The Resilient Clinician*, 2008), but self-nurturance is tied to a sense of full awareness that can be seeded in addressing several themes that

Table 5.1 Elements of Counselor Self-Nurturance

- Having patience and knowing how to pace yourself

- Having transparency

- Being open to, and releasing, the chains of one's hurts

- Valuing freshness and feeding inner simplicity

- Helpful debriefing: Modeling stillness when confronted with intense affect and immature motivations within ourselves

- Employing rituals of inner renewal

- Wasting less energy on being judgmental

- Having an appreciation of personal gifts as well as related growing edges at any given point

- Enjoying knowing, expanding, and deepening one's psychological talents

- Accepting the reality of constant change, including so-called negative experiences

- Recognizing immature motivations and counselor reactions while welcoming them home for understanding and modification

- Seeing unproductive views and behavior for what they are and addressing them accordingly

- Uncovering the lies and distortions we tell ourselves about counseling, especially when the session or therapy doesn't seem to be going well

- Being continually grateful for the wonder, awe, and joy of being a counselor

will improve both mindfulness and reflective, as opposed to reactive, living. Although many topics could naturally be noted, several stand out (see Table 5.1).

To appreciate these elements fully, there is a need for attention to self-care as well as self-knowledge, and a desire to maximize one's resiliency range. Accomplishing this goal primarily requires a spirit of *unlearning* rather than a desire to simply access existing knowledge (as important as this also is). Self-care is fairly straightforward if we follow what we set out to be needed (see the Self-Care Protocol Questionnaire for Clinicians). However, following the self-care protocol we have developed requires a form of true self-knowledge that appreciates our own resistance, confronts our own habits, and encourages us to live each day with a spirit of openness that allows us to unlearn and relearn on a continual basis. Otherwise, we find ourselves out of our educational program for years, but they are not years of experience but simply years of practicing what we initially learned about being a clinician and a person.

Self-Care Protocol Questionnaire for Clinicians

Please note: This material is for your own use. Some people tend to be quick, terse, and often global in their responses. Such approaches, while natural, limit the helpfulness of completing this questionnaire to gain as full an awareness as possible of your current profile and the personal goals you plan to develop for a realistic yet appropriately balanced and rich self-care program. Consequently, in preparing this personally designed protocol, the more clear, specific, complete, imaginative, and realistic your responses are to the questions provided, the more useful the material will be in integrating it within your schedule.

1. List healthy *nutritional practices* that you currently have in place.

_____

2. What are specific, realistic ways to improve your eating and drinking (of alcoholic beverages) habits?

_____

3. What *physical exercise* do you presently get, and when is it scheduled during the week?

_____

4. What changes in your schedule in terms of time, frequency, and variety with respect to exercise do you wish to make?

_____

5. Where are the periods for reflection, quiet time, meditation, mini-breaks alone, opportunities to center yourself, and personal debriefing times now in your schedule?

_____

6. Given your personality style, family life, and work situation, what changes would you like to make in your schedule to make it more intentional and balanced with respect to processing what comes to the forefront in your time spent alone or in silence?

_____

7. How much, what type, and how deeply and broadly do you read at this point?

_____

(*continued*)

8. What would you like to do to increase the variety or depth in your reading, research, and continuing education pursuits?

9. List activities present in your nonworking schedule not previously noted. Alongside of the frequency/time, list changes to this schedule that you feel would further enrich you personally/professionally as well as have a positive effect on your family, colleagues, and overall social network.

Activities	Frequency/Time Now Allotted	Planned Change/ Improvement
Leisure Time With:		
Spouse		
Significant Other		
Children		
Parents		
Family Members		
Friends		
Going to Movies		
Watching TV		
Visiting Museums		
Sports		
Attending Concerts/Plays		
Listening to Music		

Hiking, Biking, Walking, or Swimming		
Phone Calls to Family and Friends		
Hobbies (Gardening, coin collecting, . . .)		
Dinner Out		
Shopping		
Visiting Libraries, Bookstores, Coffee Shops		
Emailing Friends		
Making Love		
Journaling		
Continuing Education		
Vacations		
Long Weekends Away		
Meditation/Reflection/ Sitting Zazen		
Religious Rituals		
Leisurely Baths		
Massage		
Other Activities Not Listed Above:		

(*continued*)

10. What are the ways you process strong emotions (e.g., anger, anxiety, deep sadness, confusion, fear, emotional highs, or the desire to violate boundaries for reasons of personal/sexual/financial/power gratifications)?

_____

11. Where in your schedule do you regularly undertake such emotional processing?

_____

12. What would you like to do to change the extent and approaches you are now using for self-analysis/debriefing of self?

_____

13. Who serves as the interpersonal anchors in your life?

_____

14. What do you feel is lacking in your network of friends?

_____

15. What are some reasonable initiatives you wish to undertake to have a richer network?

_____

16. What are your sleep/rest habits now?

_____

17. If you are not getting enough sleep/rest, what are some realistic ways to ensure that you get more?

_____

Note: This is just a partial questionnaire. Please feel free to include, analyze, and develop a plan for improvement and integration of other aspects of self-care. Also, review your answers at different points to see what resistances to change come up and how you can face them in new creative ways by yourself or with the help of a friend, colleague, mentor, or professional counselor or therapist.

Source: Wicks, R. (2008). *The Resilient Clinician*. New York: Oxford University Press. Used with permission. Robertjwicks.com

For instance, in reviewing the points listed in Table 5.1, it is easy to say, "Well, I know these things." Yet, when we do say that, what we really are communicating is, "I know these things as I have always known them." When this is our response, no matter how educated and wise we may be, we need to honestly confront ourselves with the question: Where is the room left to see essential topics on self-nurturance in a more dynamic way given the past growth and a deepening of the wisdom we have gained along the way?

Wisdom comes about when we take knowledge and add humility, but humility is not possible without a willingness to unlearn so something new can be entertained—even about concepts, themes, and philosophies of living that we have known well in the past.

PATIENCE AND KNOWING HOW TO PACE YOURSELF

Too often we don't demonstrate the same patience with ourselves that we have with our clients. Yet, lessons take their own time to grow and ripen. Moreover, errors and acts of hypocrisy are all part of the learning process if we face them correctly.

For new counselors, in particular, but certainly not exclusively, there are so many fresh challenges to be encountered as they begin clinical practice after graduation. For instance, counselors are called to integrate everything that comes their way, including a new profession, teammates, clients, as well as a myriad of less obvious things. The journey can be overwhelming at times. Sometime during the first several years of practice it may seem to new counselors that they are merely treading water or that they are on a psychological roller-coaster ride. So, as new counselors (and at times when you are more seasoned), among other things, you must remember to do the following:

- *Pace yourself.* The beauty of new practitioners is represented in the energy and enthusiasm they have for their work. However, effort must be made to ensure there are always embers to keep that fire lit. There must be enough "psychological and spiritual oxygen" so the body can breathe deeply and the soul can sing.
- *Give yourself permission to redefine success.* Understand your original motivations to become a counselor and the success you fantasized about and then prune, prune, prune.
- *Be faithful in the moment with your clients.* Practicing mindfulness with your clients during the very short time they are actually in your presence helps this to occur more often than in most clinical and nonclinical situations.

- *Be mindful in your own life.* Having a mindfulness practice—both formal and informal—that you are involved in by yourself and, if possible, at times with others helps this to be so.
- Have a clear understanding of both your signature strengths and growing edges as a person and counselor.

TRANSPARENCY

True ordinariness allows us to enjoy and share a wonderful sense of personal energy that pumping up our ego would normally exhaust. The power of therapeutic presence becomes greater when we are not tired and tied down by defenses and postures that sap us of vitality and make us opaque, which then psychologically poisons the space we have available for our clients as well.

Author and naturalist-explorer Peter Matthiessen (1986) writes in his fascinating journal, *Nine-Headed Dragon River*:

> "The mind of a Buddha," [Roshi] Yasutani once said, "is like water that is calm, deep, and crystal clear, and upon which 'the moon of truth' reflects fully and perfectly. The mind of the ordinary man, on the other hand, is like murky water, constantly being churned by the gales of delusive thought and no longer able to reflect the moon of truth. The moon nonetheless shines steadily upon the waves, but as the waters are roiled, we are unable to see its reflection. Thus we lead lives that are frustrating and meaningless. . . .
>
> "So long as the winds of thought continue to disturb the water of our Self-nature, we cannot distinguish truth from untruth. It is imperative, therefore, that these winds be stilled. Once they abate, the waves subside, the

muddiness clears, and we perceive directly that the moon of truth has never ceased shining. The moment of such realization is . . . enlightenment, the apprehension of the true substance of our Self-nature. Unlike moral and philosophical concepts, which are variable, true Insight is imperishable." (p. 43)

As I read these words, I recalled an experience I had that was like this, which I had initially partially grasped but not fully understood until recently. It happened during a visit to Japan, where I was asked to lecture to an English-speaking group of caregivers and then to present a public lecture through an interpreter.

After completing my work, I was given a special opportunity. I took the bullet train away from the urban areas to visit a Shinto shrine at Ise Jingu. Part of the uniqueness of this visit was that I was given a personal guided tour by the director of the grounds, who many years ago had once been a simple care woodsman.

As he walked me around with my interpreter, who had also at one point been a teacher of his children, the temple grounds director stopped atop a small, slightly arched wooden bridge, looked and pointed down, and asked me, "What do you see?" After a few moments I replied, "Clear fresh water at peace." In response, he smiled, looked at me directly through his deep brown eyes, and said "Hai." He then added, "Now, what do you hear?" to which I replied, "the sound of a frog." Ahso, he remarked and then said, "You will not hear this species of frog anywhere else on the temple ground." And when I asked why, he replied, "Because this species of frog only lives near water that is clear, fresh, and at peace."

He then smiled and looked at me in a way that I knew we weren't speaking simply about water and frogs. Instead, we were speaking about my own Self, a sense of mindfulness, and the gift of real clarity, awareness, and openness it would bring me as I related to myself and the world. The implied additional question given my profession also was: Would I have this awareness or would I—and the clients I was called to help—miss what a sense of presence and openness would have to offer. It was up to me.

OPENNESS TO, AND THE RELEASE OF, THE CHAINS OF YOUR HURTS

Unfinished business often comes disguised as our friends. It tells us we have been entitled, but not given enough, that we are valuable but unappreciated and misunderstood, committed but unheeded. Yet, when we chain ourselves to our past hurts, obviously good doesn't come of it. The problem is this disguise can affect us even more as counselors.

When we become frustrated with a client who has borderline personality disorder, for instance, we may be forgetting that it is not about us and the client is doing the best he or she can under the circumstances. When this occurs, we are involving ourselves in parallel process because our frustration caused by our own unrealistic expectations mirrors those of the client, though naturally to a lesser degree.

Because we are usually in the counseling role, it takes a degree of humility to look at how our own past is affecting our present situation. Again, our attitude is the key. If we look at countertransferences as something bad, then we will want to deny, avoid, or embrace them in ways that are not helpful (i.e., self-blame). On the other hand, if we look at them with a sense of intrigue, the results can be strikingly positive. "Come home" is the call of all spiritualities; it is probably also the call of most psychologies. Certainly, it is where the counselors must be in themselves if they are to help others with their own inner work.

By welcoming home our growing edges, defenses, overinvolvement in our own ego, and characterological styles (that result in our habitually making the same mistakes) we are on the road to becoming not only better counselors but also happier, more integrated persons. Knowing that this will be a lifelong journey will also help in this regard. As a result, we will appreciate that one minute we are the wise clinician with a well-integrated ego, whereas the next we are someone who is rigid, defensive, and unaware of our negative percepts and resultant behavior. That is a reality. What isn't a reality sometimes for us is our willingness to step back and see such cognitions, behaviors, and feelings for what they are. Being a counselor doesn't insulate us from this happening; it may even result in us being equipped with more sophisticated defenses to prevent us from seeing areas in which we are closed to new knowledge.

The receptionist at a clinic once shared with me how upset she was with the treatment she received from one of the counselors. She was shocked by it. "How can she behave that way? She is a counselor!" And, she meant it. She was totally flummoxed by the counselor's behavior. A few months later, that counselor came up to me and asked for a recommendation for counseling because she was distraught by the rejection she was experiencing throughout her life. I did give her a few names and added, "Hearing your sadness I feel badly that you are going through all of this. I am glad you are treating yourself to some counseling at this tender time in your life. I hope you get the support you need but also the development of a relationship that releases you to tenderly but clearly look at yourself since as you know as a counselor the power resides in us, not those with whom we have not found a satisfactory interpersonal relationship." I felt I could share that with her since we had worked side-by-side and shared clinical problems and had a pretty good relationship. The balance of clarity and kindness is always crucial in how we share our reflections and also how we confront ourselves.

VALUING FRESHNESS AND FEEDING INNER SIMPLICITY THROUGH GREATER MINDFULNESS

When we are open and welcoming to each moment, it gives us the permission to move to new vantage points in our life; different awareness than the formulations of the past can then come to the fore and equip us better to meet today. Zen Master Shunryu Suzuki was once asked to define Zen in a few words. When this happened, everyone in the room laughed because of the tall order of the request. However, when the laughter died down, he simply responded: "Everything changes" (Chadwick, 1999).

Cognitive constructs that we form are helpful, but as guides. Openness to change is really a college of mindfulness. We can learn when we suspend judgment and simply—but unfortunately not easily—experience what and who are in front of us in our clinical practice and life. Inner simplicity can help uncover when our habits and fears are interfering with such an openness to flowing with the movements of our life if we truly honor this state.

Maitland (1998), in her book on her experience and love of silence, relates how simplicity became more and more appreciated as she moved through her life:

> I began to recognize that silence and simplicity do have a connection. I found myself immensely encouraged and influenced by Henry Thoreau . . . and have increasingly adopted . . . his economic theory. . . . [W]e should not calculate our wealth by how much we had or owned, but by how much free time we have. How much time there is left over when our needs have been met is the best measure of wealth. This means of course, that the less you need the richer you are. . . . I started asking myself about

> everything I thought about buying not, "Can I afford this?" but "Am I prepared to spend x hours working at something less interesting than silence in order to have it?" (p. 262)

Enslavement to so many things becomes evident to us as persons and counselors when we allow the psychological "dust" (inner and outer activities) to settle during periods of alonetime. As counselors we begin to see not only attachments to things but also to such desires as a wish to voyeuristically enter (rather than helpfully explore) other people's lives; to be in a role of prestige, power, respect, and control; to receive feedback from clients that we are brilliant, attractive, amazingly helpful, or wise. Being mindful, having a basic style of interacting with clients, and seeing (but not excusing, rationalizing, or being extremely hard on ourselves) when we step out of this style, and valuing inner and outer simplicity can be helpful in avoiding pitfalls in seeking self-knowledge or crossing boundaries.

In Pico Iyer's (2003) book on the Dalai Lama, he writes:

> He really does live simply, decorating his bedroom when he travels with just a few pictures of his teachers and his family, and a portable radio. He really is a full-time, life-long student of the Buddha, who taught him that nearly everything is illusory and passing. . . . And he really does aspire, as every monk does, to a simplicity that lies not before complexity but on the far side of it, having not dodged experience but subsumed it. (p. 19)

Although as counselors we are not monks, some of the lessons of simplicity are worth emulating in ways such as:

- Having a theme or mission for our counseling approach and our life as a whole
- Being aware of our gifts, when we use them to help others and when they are employed in the service of our ego instead of compassion
- Knowing each day about the fragility of life and the reality of impermanence
- Paying attention to what you are doing now and who is before you

HELPFUL PERSONAL DEBRIEFING: MODELING STILLNESS WHEN CONFRONTED WITH OUR EMOTIONS AND IMMATURE MOTIVATIONS

One of the gifts we give our clients is to respond by reflecting rather than reacting when intense emotion fills the room. When the fire is between the clients and us, we explore it with them until the fire dies down and there are only ashes left. Following that, we then ask them how what was experienced in the room has been experienced elsewhere in their life. In doing this, we both model and teach our clients about self-regulation and how to debrief oneself.

However, such a debriefing of emotions also needs to be done when the emotions are *within* us as counselors—maybe even more so given our work. All counselors experience such states or reactions as physical and emotional exhaustion, feelings of anxiety that the client is not getting better or wants to change therapists, boredom with what the person is sharing, or even, if we are honest, with whom the client is and the problem being presented, and hypersensitivity because the client is able to zero in on our own unfinished business, lack of knowledge, or personal issues.

At the end of the day, a counter-transferential review (Wicks, 2008) can help in this regard. This would include basic questions that would help us put our fingers on the pulse of our emotions:

- What made me sad?
- What overwhelmed me?
- What sexually aroused me?
- What made me extremely happy or even confused me? (p. 31)

In looking at ourselves during a quiet period at the end of the day in our office or during the ride or walk home, much wonderful information can be surfaced from which to learn.

EMPLOYING RITUALS OF INNER RENEWAL

Each morning, I begin my day with a ritual that has proved to be an anchor for me in both joyful and challenging times. I rise at an early hour, make coffee, and sit propped up in bed for about a half hour. This time allows me to slowly awaken, appreciate the joy of being alive, and to center myself for the day ahead.

Any thoughts that arise, I let move through me like a train. I don't stop the thought train, hop on, or indulge the issue that comes up but merely notice it nonjudgmentally. It can be faced or possibly solved later. I just smile at it and recall the peace of early morning with gratitude for being alive. After about half an hour is over, or on occasion longer, my wife awakes and I get another coffee for myself and one for her. We chat and eventually watch the morning news before our day begins. This second part of the ritual opens up space for and between us before we are bombarded with all the day's events and experiences.

For some counselors, maybe during or at the end of the day, a time for such a ritual would be good. However, no matter when such times that allow us to stop, breathe, and enjoy come about, they are essential because they provide an antidote to the temptation to rush through our lives in a cognitive cocoon while deluding ourselves all the while that, if we are honest, what we are doing is only practical, and that is what life is really about for all of us.

Other simple but potentially powerful rituals might include:

- Walking in the morning, at lunch, during a break or client cancellation, or at the end of the workday
- Setting aside periods for reading, playing a game, listening to music, watching a favorite show on television, chatting with a friend, enjoying a cup of tea or glass of cool water, gardening, emailing your thoughts about something dear to you, or a hobby
- Practicing meditation
- Involving yourself in activities you simply flow with
- Journaling or writing
- Researching areas you find fascinating
- Preparing something—possibly a meal—with a sense of care and love
- Taking a leisurely bath

There are so many rituals that renew. What other ones come to mind for you?

WASTING LESS ENERGY ON BEING JUDGMENTAL

In the book, *The Mindful Way Through Depression*, Williams, Teasdale, Segal, and Kabat-Zinn (2007) discuss how persons can free themselves from chronic unhappiness through the way they face all of life—even the negative. The same information can be directed at us as counselors in what and how we greet aspects of our life that we don't like.

Some of their suggestions and reflections provided throughout the book that are worth considering when adapted to our role as counselors include:

- Being curious with respect to our feelings during sessions as well as throughout the rest of our day
- Responding to negative emotions with a questioning air rather than simply with aversion, retreat, or attack tactics
- Searching for real facts about negative situations rather than automatically embracing without question our current evaluations and explanations for such feelings
- Exploring more fully what is actually happening while being careful not to siphon off energy into what *should* be happening
- Paying attention in a way that we see more of the reality rather than only our reality at the moment and enjoying the process of being intrigued rather than judging ourselves or others or being upset that we can't be more naturally mindful. (After all, mindfulness isn't a contest, though even this attitude can be distorted by our ego and a spirit of competition.)

At the very least, such approaches as these and other ones included in books on mindfulness can result in our wasting less energy and enjoying more of our life and clinical practice.

For instance, if clients are chronically late, interrupt you when you are summarizing, or get annoyed when you provide feedback that requires them to consider something in a new way, there may be a tendency to react inside with frustration, annoyance, or another unpleasant response. When this occurs, you may feel that this response is natural. However, why do we leave such an automatic reaction unchallenged? Such judgmental thoughts and feelings only sap our limited energy.

In supervision, I suggest that the next time this occurs, why not tease or laugh at yourself for your instant negative reaction. The false judgmental self does not like to be laughed at, so this negative, draining response will—once confronted that way—have a chance to atrophy so inner space can be opened up to be intrigued about why the client is initiating such an unproductive attitude. As counselors, we deal with a great amount of intensity, so conserving our energy can be a great boon to us and those we treat.

HAVING AN APPRECIATION OF PERSONAL GIFTS AS WELL AS RELATED GROWING EDGES AT ANY GIVEN POINT

When I work with new counselors I have them make a list of their personal and professional gifts. The goal of this exercise involves:

- Being aware of what they have to put at the service of their clients
- Having a greater sense of—in the language of positive psychology—what their signature strengths are to enjoy in their personal lives
- Becoming more aware of how their defenses and growing edges are related to their talents since one's very gifts tend to become one's problems under certain circumstances

- Appreciating the greater freedom that is achieved when we can enjoy our gifts and have our defenses atrophy if we can assess ourselves accurately rather than in an inflated or deflated way
- Uncovering or recognizing more clearly the sources available for such information about our style and the topography of our personality

The sources for such information for counseling students and new clinicians might include the psychological testing they have experienced as part of their graduate education, their own therapy, clinical feedback in small groups as well as in their classes, course readings, and comments from friends, family, and associates, as well as from clinical supervision in their field placements.

As counselors who have been practicing for awhile, those sources might be dated, so instead of or in addition to what information was provided to them as students and beginning practitioners, there is also:

- Peer supervision
- Journaling at the end of the day about one's objective experiences and the subjective responses made to them
- Informal feedback by family, friends, and co-workers
- Reflections during and after reading works in psychology and spirituality
- Review of positive psychology books to ensure one has an up-to-date, comprehensive list of personal and professional gifts as well as an understanding of the situations in which their gifts became distorted or eliminated because of certain situations that keyed off defensive responses

SEEING UNPRODUCTIVE VIEWS AND BEHAVIORS FOR WHAT THEY ARE AND ADDRESSING THEM ACCORDINGLY

There are also numerous behaviors and views that we recognize as counselors in ourselves and others that are unproductive. Some of the more obvious ones that are worth recalling are:

- In the process of taking your clients and clinical work seriously, you take a detour and take yourself too seriously instead.
- Scheduling clients back to back with no space to take a breath; instead, psychologically decontaminate yourself and prepare for your next session at a leisurely pace.
- Develop a style of living that is not in line with the guidelines you offer clients, family, and friends.
- Failure to carefully diagnose situations that result in you demonstrating a "tyranny of hope" that runs the risk of having goals for clients that are impossible/impractical for them to reach given their personal and other resources.
- Failure in sessions to both appreciate and self-regulate negative emotions arising from issues or situations from one's early or current personal life.
- Having no process to notice and examine trends in workaholism, ongoing fatigue, emotional distance, or overidentification with clients, and making sharp or—at the other end of the spectrum—flat/cynical/intellectualized responses.

With an attitude marked by openness, intrigue, and hopefulness, all of these attitudes/responses need not be the last word. Rather, once again, when we observe and minimize self-condemnation and projection, rather than discouragement being the result, there is a greater opportunity to learn and go deeper.

Kornfield (1993) helps us to understand unproductive responses to what crosses our path in life when he asks:

How have I treated this difficulty so far?
How have I suffered by my own response and reaction to it?
What does this problem ask me to let go of?
What suffering is unavoidable, is my measure to accept?
What great lessons might it be able to teach me?
What is gold, the value, hidden in this situation? (p. 81)

With respect to our clinical work, by mindfully and continually examining our failures in particular, not only will those we treat benefit, but our lives will be more rewarding as well. More specifically, we will find:

- Our approach to challenges will be marked with less discouragement and greater intellectual curiosity, willingness to change course if needed, and an interest in bringing to bear new information on both our life and our practice.
- A sense of gratitude that we can involve ourselves in a formal and informal reflective process each day
- A new commitment and openness to creativity regarding how we meet clients, ourselves, and life so potential knowledge for how we can live now can be embraced
- A better sense of what we can change and what we can't
- Increasing our understanding of what it means to fail mindfully so energy is placed at the service of understanding rather than defense

- A greater recognition that as we balance our life as a counselor and person involved in so many renewing and depleting activities, we can have a greater sensitivity to what stressors may be present, how to recognize them early, and know the healthiest attitude and approach to bounce back and learn from their presence.

BEING CONTINUALLY GRATEFUL FOR THE WONDER, AWE, AND JOY OF BEING A COUNSELOR

There is no doubt that being a counselor isn't easy. After all, who wants to be in a profession where people unconsciously seek to undermine the process or want to share their depression, face the counselor with the sad realities of sexual, physical, spiritual, or psychological abuse, scare the counselor by being suicidal or threatening to others, bombard the person trying to help them with their stress and anxiety, drain them with their manic episodes, parse words and motives and make unreasonable borderline demands, as well as act out in ways that require constant follow-up to get financial recompense for the sessions.

Top this off with clients changing counselors, prematurely terminating, threatening to sue, the overall intensity of counseling periodically forcing the counselors' own unresolved issues to the surface, thus adding to their own age-related and societal pressures (i.e., financial recession), and the natural question that surfaces is: Why did I ever become a counselor or stay in this profession given all the stress it places on me?

Well, just as the list of challenges is extensive, so are the rewards. Being a counselor is truly like being in treatment yourself for your whole life since you are dealing with both the process and content of what makes life good for people. If counseling is done in the right spirit though, with good support and informal or formal supervision, and a sense that it is a wisdom profession that can even transform failure into something that makes life deeper and better, this profession can bring joy and fulfillment equal to the richest vocations in the world. For instance, being a counselor sets the stage for the possibility of the following:

- Recognizing the importance and value of moving from emphasis on the extrinsic to the intrinsic and from projection to embracing everything with an eye to self-understanding
- Becoming less judgmental and more filled with a spirit of intrigue—even about one's failures and so-called negative experiences so one can better see how to improve as a clinician
- Deepening an appreciation of one's own value system
- Having a stage on which to improve and broaden one's psychological awareness and skills
- Appreciating the inner workings of many different types of people
- Having an opportunity to increase, apply, and enjoy one's interpersonal skills
- Being honored with a chance to hear people's intimate, powerful, and poignant stories with an eye toward enabling them to expand their story of themselves through the treatment process
- Experiencing people's pilgrimage toward greater integration while having the chance to uncover and release the energy being held captive by their past history and current limiting schemata

- Accepting the constancy of change and the need for flexibility, openness, and creativity in order to accommodate it into both one's clinical practice and personal life
- Seeing the need for and becoming more willing to be transparent
- Replacing therapeutic formulae with fresh, mindful responses to what the client is presenting

Yet, for such joys to manifest themselves, as counselors we must be willing to continually learn. For this to occur, having both alonetime and excellent mentors to help us more fully appreciate the space in our inner life (as well as to learn to be mentors ourselves) are necessary.

6

—————⟫•◇•⟨—————

Alonetime as a University: Honoring the Wisdom of Mentors of Mindfulness

A s counselors, it would be foolish not to emulate some of the primary facets of the apprenticeship relationship as either the guide or the person seeking some direction. We need help to create the psychological and spiritual room to let go of what is unnecessary and destructive in life and welcome what is good and freeing. No matter what final form the relationship takes today, it should not be taken lightly, so we must:

1. Be committed to act—not just desire or talk about change
2. Know why we are seeking such a psychologically costly mentoring relationship
3. Appreciate what contemporary wisdom figures should truly be like when we are prepared to take the significant step to seek one or are asked to be such a presence to others

In examining these three points, we will also see that there are key elements from an array of spiritual traditions upon which we can draw to illustrate them.

COMMITMENT TO ACT

A *rinpoche* (teacher) from the Tibetan Buddhist tradition notes, "When you see a person who is, as you say, enlightened, and you wish you would be able to attain these qualities, it is very important that you put this wish into action" (Johnson, 1996). Too often people spend their whole adult lives just musing how nice it would be to have a highly trusted mentor with whom they could share their life in a transparent way. Instead of perpetually musing on this desire, we need to follow through with it to be open with someone wiser than we are.

Although we owe a mentor or guide a great deal of respect, we still need to be careful about idol worship. We must keep our eye on the ultimate goal and not on the spiritual guide we believe can help us get there. As the first great poet in the history of haiku, Matsuo Basho, said, "Do not seek to follow in the footsteps of men of old, seek what they sought."

Once we are willing to act, the next step is to have the most serious commitment to become involved in the process. We must continue to be faithful to it, and not step back—no matter what! To navigate all of this with effort, intensity, and faithfulness is not easy. As writer, photographer, and activist Walter Lippman clearly appreciates, "To want salvation cheap, and most men do, there is very little comfort to be had out of a great teacher" (source unknown). For instance, even when we do feel a sense of being drawn into a mentoring relationship—one maybe we have even possibly sought for years—the hesitation to take advantage of the gift of finding a true teacher and becoming fully involved with this wise figure may still be there.

We can see this paradox of intimacy in Andrew Harvey's (1983) spiritual classic, *Journey in Ladakh*. Speaking of a Tibetan *rinpoche*, one businessperson who was also an impetuous spiritual seeker shares the following impression with Harvey as to why he thinks his guide is different: "He makes you feel immediately at home with him. He does not want anything from you. He is tender to all the people around him. . . . You feel seen by him" (p. 125). But later he also confesses: "Men like him are [also quite] frightening. They are so clear they make you feel dirty. For the last twenty years I have been wanting to meet a man like him—and when I did, the first thing I wanted to do was leave. . . ." (p. 135).

So, even before approaching a spiritual master or sage, we must be willing and appreciative of what is involved. In a previous work (Wicks, 1992), I outlined four factors that are important to remember when we seek out a spiritual guide or mentor:

1. We only seek such special assistance when there is a real need and we have already utilized and found somewhat wanting all existing supports in our lives, including our own personal resources (i.e., problem solving, reflection, prayer).

2. We need to be serious in our request for information and not just inquisitive (some people are continually asking for "a word" from these spiritual figures without weighing the gravity of their request).

3. Take special care in selecting someone who we feel will be of real benefit to us *now*. There is an old Russian proverb that states: "The hammer shatters glass but forges steel." A sage who can be of real help to one person at certain junctures in life may be of no assistance to him or her at another point or be of no help at all to other types of individuals who seek help. . . .

4. Recognize that we might not like, or immediately understand what we are told. . . . Even the best mentors have many persons who came to them who do not react positively to their answers to their questions. (p. 119)

Although a relationship like this offers the hope of a path to peace and joy, entering into such a relationship is not to be taken lightly. There must be willingness to deal with questions and suggestions that will be taxing at times. We must be honest, open, and sometimes even courageous and strong. Again, a desert story makes this clear.

> Abba Sisoes the Theban requested of his disciple, "Tell me what you see in me and in turn I will tell you what I see in you."
>
> His disciple said to him: "You are good in spirit but a little harsh."
>
> The old man said in reply: "You are good in spirit too but your soul is not tough enough." (author's translation)

WHY SEEK SUCH A PSYCHOLOGICALLY COSTLY RELATIONSHIP?

Clearly, the road to uncovering and embracing wisdom in our lives is not an easy one. It is natural for us to wonder, given all the effort and potentially painful experiences of being mentored, why we would ever want a disciple-type relationship? There are several reasons for making such a commitment. One is that there is a deep desire to be with someone with whom we can be ourselves: sharing joys and sadness, doubts and convictions, shames and proud moments, questions and philosophies. But underneath all of this is a simple need to re-experience one's life with all of its wishes, fears, anger, impulses, and past significant relationships.

The goal is to re-create one's life, to emotionally, cognitively, and behaviorally restructure the way one journeys through life along more personally satisfying lines. The belief is that as an apprentice I will be able to borrow from the strength as well as the philosophy of someone whom I trust. As an apprentice I believe that my guide is living more authentically and peacefully than others. As a result, by being faithful to the lessons I am taught through word and modeling I can do the same—albeit in a different, maybe lesser, way. As is the case of many types of spiritual and psychological mentoring, the relationship is crucial. This very interpersonal connection enables a person to choose differently, act more wisely, and finally make progress rather than being caught in a web of old habits.

We can see this thinking in the Zen tradition quite clearly. In *Benedict's Dharma* (Henry, 2001), Judith Simmer-Brown shares that:

> When I first met my root teacher, Venerable Chogyam Trungpa Rinpoche, I asked why a personal teacher was necessary. He answered, "It is because we tend to be too hard on ourselves." If we have a personal teacher who can really see us, it is possible to give up torturing ourselves unnecessarily. In my relationship with Rinpoche, I was often embarrassed because he would see my confusion and self-absorption so clearly, but even more I was constantly overwhelmed by his warmth and compassion toward me. (p. 97)

Still, the essential questions remain:

- Who will serve as this person?
- What traits does one seek in such an individual?
- Are there commonalities among helpers that it would be beneficial to know about when seeking out someone like this?

Knowing and finding the right type of person to guide us can make all the difference. Although the relationship is not the only condition for change, it is certainly a *necessary* condition if significant progress in strengthening our inner life is to become a reality. Similarly, if we are able to be a guide for others in either a formal or (as is more often the case) informal way, then we must also be aware of how we are to accompany people seeking a new life.

WHAT ARE THESE PEOPLE LIKE?

The ancient spiritual *abbas* (Fathers) and *ammas* (Mothers) had many traits or gifts that contemporary guides should seek to possess. However, for our purposes, I would like to briefly focus on several traits that appear to be essential, especially given the intensity that a mentor-apprentice relationship may exhibit at times. From my own experience and study, the wisdom of different world religions seems to indicate that it is important that guides:

- Offer acceptance and space to those who seek their assistance
- Possess an encouraging and contagious holiness
- Exemplify extraordinariness, humility, transparency, and practicality
- Offer perspective, especially in the darkness
- Demonstrate the paradox of possibility and challenge
- Are un-self-conscious
- Are able to be at home in the now
- Do not seek answers as much as ways to live more completely with the questions
- Do not get in the way of the message, remove the person's ultimate independence, or interfere with the person's unique movement toward greater freedom

Because these traits are so rarely seen today, is it any wonder that finding or becoming such a guide is so challenging? Though this is the case, we must not step back from the call to seek and be what is necessary. There are people like this in the world. In addition, we can and should seek to be like those we admire. We may never reach their spiritual maturity, but it doesn't really matter. What is important is that we strive to be of solace and support to those who ask for our help in the best way we can. Spending some time reflecting on the essential qualities of a spiritual guide is a sound next step.

OFFERS ACCEPTANCE AND SPACE TO THOSE SEEKING THEIR ASSISTANCE

I remember once being with a spiritual guide and thinking "I don't think I aged when I was with him!" Aging takes friction, and he was so nondefensive and nonthreatening that I felt like I flowed through time. I am sure that if I criticized him, he would have responded: "Why, yes. Those are some of my faults. How observant of you to notice." He was an amazing person who had no need for unnecessary defenses and posturing. He was extraordinary and didn't waste energy on defensiveness, but instead had it at his disposal for his own search for self-knowledge as well as the teaching of others like myself who are so bound by our own ego and negative or inadequate training.

The space Desert Fathers and Mothers of the Fourth Century offered came from the inner space that is reflected in their humility. Such people are ones who embrace solitude and are comfortable with silence. Their gifts also are contagious for those who are open enough to receive the *charisms* that allow them to be in the world with a sense of true spontaneity, freedom, and purity of heart.

POSSESS AN ENCOURAGING AND CONTAGIOUS APPEAL

Mitch Albom (1997), in his best-selling book, *Tuesdays with Morrie*, admitted, "When I visited Morrie I liked myself better" (p. 55). I think he made these statements because there was a unique sense of presence in a true spiritual and psychological mentor, which is, in itself, transformative. Jeffrey Kottler (1986) addresses this quality of presence in terms of psychotherapy and counseling. His insights remind us that while wisdom figures and helpers create a quality of presence, people also have great expectations of them when they seek help:

> Lock a person, any person, in a room alone with Sigmund Freud, Carl Rogers, Fritz Perls, Albert Ellis, or any formidable personality and several hours later he will come out different. It is not what the therapist does that is important . . . but rather who she is. A therapist who is vibrant, inspirational, charismatic, who is sincere, loving and nuturing, who is wise, confident, and self-disciplined will have a dramatic affect by the sheer force and power of her essence. . . .
>
> The first and foremost element of change then is the therapist's presence—his excitement, enthusiasm, and the power of his personality. . . . The therapist enters the relationship with clarity, openness, and serenity and comes fully prepared to encounter a soul in torment. The client comes prepared with his own expectations for a mentor, a doctor, a friend, or a wizard. (n. p.)

True guides are people who teach us even more by who they are than by what they know. They are people who enable us to feel that change, *profound* change, in us is possible, because of our encounter with them. This can be said about anyone filling a teaching role or a mentoring position. For instance, William James said of college professors, "Organization and method mean much, but contagious human characters mean even more in a university" (source unknown). It is no mere coincidence that his brother, the author Henry James, expressed the following similar sentiment: "A teacher affects eternity, he can never tell where his influence stops" (source unknown).

The presence of contagious emptiness (according to Buddhists) or holiness (Judeo-Christian and Hindu thinking) not only creates a feeling of support, but it also calls us to be open to experience a sense of presence in a unique way in our own lives. In this way, apprenticeship can have a positive ripple effect leading to a stronger spiritual community. Some years ago, Archbishop Desmond Tutu of South Africa was addressing the divinity students at General Theological Seminary. About halfway through his presentation, one of the seminarians in the audience nudged the dean of the seminary who was sitting next to him, pointed up at the stage, and said, "Desmond Tutu is a holy man." In response the dean asked, "How do you know that he is holy?" To this the seminarian didn't even blink. Instead, after a brief pause, he replied, "I know that Desmond Tutu is holy because when I am with Desmond Tutu, *I* feel holy." Can the same be said of us by those who we encounter in our daily lives?

The overall challenge, even when being an apprentice, is to simultaneously ask ourselves specific, potentially revealing questions such as: How do people feel when we are with them? Do they feel the same space of love and freedom given to us by our *ammas* and *abbas*? Or, instead, do they feel our need to control, our desire to be appreciated or followed, our need to be liked or seen as bright, attractive, wise, or spiritual? Do they feel this openness and place of safety where they can rest their doubts, problems, and concerns, or do they feel our own anxiety, stress, and defensiveness? What do they feel? If we are filled with ourselves or the desire to be famous, powerful, even effective (as enjoyable and beneficial as having this wish granted may be), then we lack the essential ingredient, either *humility*, *ordinariness*, or (in some traditions) *emptiness*.

EXEMPLIFY EXTRAORDINARINESS, HUMILITY, AND PRACTICALITY

There is a power in true desert *ammas* and *abbas* that comes from their extraordinariness. Trudy Dixon said about Zen Master Shunryu Suzuki:

> The qualities of his life are extraordinary—buoyancy, vigor, straightforwardness, simplicity, humility, joyfulness, uncanny perspicacity . . . but in the end it is . . . the teacher's utter ordinariness [that deepens the student's appreciation of their own spirituality]. Because he is just himself, he is a mirror for his students. . . . In his presence we see our original face and the extraordinariness we see in only our own true nature. (n. p.)

Such a sense of presence is striking. Someone once said of a Benedictine priest who founded a Catholic ashram in India, "To walk into Fr. Bede [Griffiths] was like hitting a wall of holiness" (du Boulay, 1998). Such individuals have a palpable presence that can have a major effect of its own accord, particularly if the apprentice is ready. As Jack Kornfield (2000) notes in his instructive book, *After the Ecstasy, the Laundry*:

> The understanding of emptiness is contagious. It appears we can catch it from one another. We know that when a

sad or angry person enters a room, we too often enter sadness or anger. It shouldn't surprise us then, that the presence of a teacher who is empty, open, awake can have a
powerful effect on another person, especially if that person is ripe. (p. 79)

These teachers are ordinary, humble, and able to make the
teachings practical and alive because they represent the lessons
they impart. Yet they are truly "characters of wonder and awe"
because they build on the sense of magnetism they have in a way
that helps people more readily incorporate new and necessary
changes into their lives. Sogyal Rinpoche (1992), in his classic
work *The Tibetan Book of Living and Dying*, wrote:

My master, Jamyang Khyentse, was tall for a Tibetan,
and he always seemed to stand a good head above others
in a crowd. He had silver hair, cut very short, and kind
eyes that glowed with humor. His ears were long, like
those of the Buddha. But what you noticed most about
him was his presence. His glance and bearing told you he
was a wise and holy man. He had a rich, deep, enchant-
ing voice, and when he taught his head would tilt slightly
backward and the teaching would flow from him in a
stream of eloquence and poetry. And for all the respect
and even awe he commanded, there was humility in
everything he did. . . . With his warmth and wisdom and
compassion, he personified the sacred truth of the teachings and so made them practical and vibrant with life.
(pp. xi, xii)

The sense of practicality and common sense Sogyal Rinpoche
refers to with respect to his own Master is unfortunately uncommon today. It is a mark of spiritual wisdom that can have a direct

effect on a person's life. This is not a new insight. For ages it has been recognized that true wisdom is applicable even across centuries. In his Introduction to his book on *Desert Wisdom*, which chronicles the wisdom of fourth- and fifth-century hermits, contemplative Merton (1960) emphasizes this for us:

> These words of the Fathers are never theoretical in our modern sense of the word. They are never abstract. They deal with concrete things and jobs to be done in the everyday life of a fourth century monk. But what is said serves just as well for a [modern] thinker. The basic realities of the interior life are there: faith, humility, charity, meekness, discretion, self-denial. But not the least of these qualities of the "words of salvation" is their common sense. (p. 13)

And nowhere is this common sense and the concrete, practical advice they offered more needed than when encountering personal darkness.

OFFERS PERSPECTIVE, EVEN IN THE DARKNESS

Thich Nhat Hahn once said, "During the Vietnam War we were so busy helping the wounded that we sometimes forgot to smell the flowers. Night has a very pleasant smell in Vietnam, especially in the country. But we would forget to pay attention to the smell of mint, coriander, thyme, and sage" ("An interview with Thich Nhat Hanh," 1989). Simple statements like this serve as reminders to stay awake so we can know what gifts lie before us, especially in the most trying of times. This is important because they provide us with a new perspective and way of seeing life.

Still, what they offer is often rejected because it is contained in the seemingly paradoxical combination of possibility and difficulty. In her little book on the Buddha, Karen Armstrong (2000) wrote, "[The] life of the Buddha challenges some of our strongest convictions but it can also be a beacon. . . . His example illuminates some of the ways in which we can reach for an enhanced and more truly compassionate humanity" (pp. xxviii–xxxix).

Thomas Merton (1988) echoes this point in his published journal *A Vow of Conversation*:

> Blakham, writing of [the philosopher] Sartre, says wisely that popular wisdom easily accepts *extreme* views but not disturbing ones. The extreme view is that to live well is impossible, or the other extreme that to live well is easy: this they will readily accept. But Sartre's claim that to live well is difficult and possible, they reject as despair. (p. 10)

This is also the core of mentorship or discipleship: to live well, be free, and have purity of heart or an unobstructed vision of what is. Then we can see life clearly and completely; we can know that it is both difficult and possible much of the time. Life comes as a single package. It can't be parsed as it often is by those who seek easy answers or want an excuse to shrink from facing the essential questions and challenges that come up for everyone.

While there is always a challenge, sometimes darkness is unnecessary. Yet, with some energy, courage, and guidance from a mentor, darkness can be avoided or turned to our advantage. In a previous book of mine, *Seeds of Sensitivity* (1995), I outlined some of the kinds of darkness that are avoidable and unnecessary. They are important to remember in this context as well:

- Lack of self-awareness, self-acceptance, and self-love
- Dishonesty

- Intolerance of others
- Unfinished business with family and friends
- Suppressed/repressed negative feelings
- Poorly developed ethics, beliefs, and values
- Attachments or addictions
- Hidden, past, or unintegrated embarrassments
- Resistance to intimacy
- Failure to take care of oneself physically
- Lack of honesty and openness in prayer
- Lack of meaning in life
- Ungrieved losses
- Greed
- Unreasonable expectations of self and others
- A sense of entitlement
- Unresolved anger
- Unwillingness to risk and an inordinate need for security
- Inability to experience quiet in one's life
- Unhealthy self-involvement or, at the other extreme, lack of healthy self-interest
- Failure to set priorities in life
- Irresponsibility
- Being a perfectionist and inordinately self-critical
- Unwillingness to accept love except in ways one has pre-determined as meaningful ("if so-and-so doesn't love me then the other warmth and acceptance in my life isn't important")
- Fear of responsibility and a tendency to project blame (pp. 127–128)

There are times when inner darkness is unavoidable. Apprentices need to be helped to see this and not run away. There is always the temptation to medicate oneself with drugs, sex, work, or even prayer. It is difficult to be present to the impasse of this darkness so it can eventually give way to new learning and light. In the words of one Zen Master, when confronted by an upset disciple who was ready to give up his meditative practice, "You just try and you fail, and then you go deeper" (p. 15). Just those words enabled the distressed apprentice to remain where he needed to be: with his darkness.

A SENSE OF UN-SELF-CONSCIOUSNESS

Characters of wonder and awe also have a sense of un-self-consciousness. Their goodness flows naturally and freely, not out of a sense of duty or because of guilt. Henri Nouwen (1970) provided a fine example of this when he indicated our limitations with respect to the way we often "love" others. He said:

It is important for me to realize how limited, imperfect, and weak my understanding of love has been. . . . My idea of love proves to be exclusive: "You only love me truly if you love others less"; possessive: "If you really love me, I want you to pay special attention to me"; and manipulative: "When you love me, you will do extra things for me." Well, this idea of love easily leads to vanity: "You must see something very special in me"; to jealousy: "Why are you now suddenly so interested in someone else and not in me?"; and to anger: "I am going to let you know that you have let me down and rejected me." (p. 84)

We see similar sentiment expressed in a reflection on this spirit of un-self-consiousness given in a story by Taoist philosopher Chuang Tzu, who lived in the span between the fourth and third centuries BC:

> In an age when life on earth was full, no one paid any special attention to worthy men, nor did they single out the man of ability. Rulers were simply the highest branches on the tree, and the people were like deer in woods. They were honest and righteous without realizing that they were "doing their duty." They loved each other and did not know that they were "men to be trusted." They were reliable and did not know that this was "good faith." They lived freely together giving and taking, and did not know that they were "generous." For this reason their deeds have not been narrated. They made no history. (Merton, 1965, p. 76)

This sense of giving naturally and with no desire for anything in return is certainly in the spirit of the Desert Fathers and Mothers of the fourth and fifth centuries. Although they are especially known for what they have said about living in silence and solitude and the value of asceticism, compassion remains at the heart of what they teach. We can see this in some of their sayings, particularly the blunt one that follows:

> One brother presented an *abba* with the following situation and question:
> "There are two brothers. One of them keeps a sense of silence and solitude in his cell, fasting for six days at a time, and disciplining himself quite harshly. The other brother serves the sick. Father, of the two of them, who is more acceptable to God?"

The *abba* responded: "Even if the brother who stayed in his cell, fasting for six days, and hung himself by the nose, he would not equal the one who serves the sick." (author's translation)

ARE YOU ABLE TO BE AT HOME IN THE NOW?

Inspirational guides are able to be at home in the now as well. This is another rare trait but an essential one in a spiritual guide. Irish novelist James Joyce put it well when he said one of his characters, Mr. Duffy, "lived a short distance from his body." If we are honest with ourselves, isn't that the way most of us live much of the time? However, spiritual guides would teach us that the opposite is necessary for us to be fully alive—no matter what is going on. In his book *The Wooden Bowl*, Clark Strand (1998) said about his mentor, Deh Chun:

When I consider the years of our association, the most remarkable thing is that I cannot recall any particular thing that I learned from him. I can't point to a particular conversation we had and say, "Well you know, then Deh Chun said such and such and everything was clear." At the time *nothing* was clear. When I think back on it now, I realize that his entire teaching consisted of being in the present moment, with nothing else whatsoever added on.

Being with Deh Chun was like dropping through a hole in everything that the world said was important—education, progress, money, sex, prestige. It was like discovering that nothing else mattered and all I needed was *now*—the moment—to survive. Sitting there in the little house, listening to the water boil, to the twigs crackling in the wood stove, I was temporarily removed from the game. That was the genius of his teaching, that he could bring forth that transformation without even saying a word.

His was a state of complete simplicity. Like water, the direction of his life was downward, always seeking lower ground. (pp. 7–8)

When Strand went on to describe what Deh Chun's physical setting was, it could easily have been one that would suit a modern-day desert *abba* or *amma*:

When I met him he lived in a ramshackle two-room house heated by a wood stove the size of a typewriter. There was no furniture, only a few turned-over crates and several cardboard boxes in which he kept his clothes. His bed consisted of two sawhorses on top of which he placed a 3×5 sheet of plywood and a piece of packing foam. I remember thinking once that this bed suited him perfectly, his body was so light and small.

A similar structure in another room served as a desk for writing letters and for painting his ink-washed Chinese landscapes. Propped against the back door were spades, a shovel, and a rake, tools he used to tend a plot of land the size of two king-size beds laid end to end. With the exception of tea, soybeans, peanut butter, molasses, and occasional wheat-flour, whatever he ate came from there. . . .

Nowadays, in books on meditation, it has become standard practice to say that your teacher was a mirror that allowed you to see your true self. But that was not my experience with Deh Chun. It was more like floating weightless on the Dead Sea and looking up at an empty sky. There was a feeling of tremendous peace and freedom, but that was all. I didn't know anything after I was done. Trying to pin him down on some aspect of meditation was as pointless as trying to drive a stake through the air. He taught me one thing only, and that he taught me to perfection: meditation happens now. (pp. 7–8)

LIVING WITH THE QUESTIONS AND INSTILLING PATIENCE IN OURSELVES

True guides who will help us through our inner deserts are filled with wisdom but are not "answer people." Instead they call us to live with the questions in a different way. For instance, when questioned, one master said, "If I give you an answer you'll think you understand." Thomas Merton similarly advised, "No one can give you a map. Your terrain is unique . . . just some guidance and courage about how to handle different terrain."

Zen master Shunryu Suzuki (2002) offered a similar caution:

"If I tell you something, you will stick to it, and limit your own capacity to find out for yourself." But, as Katagiri Roshi said, "You have to say something." Because if the teacher says nothing, the students wander about sticking to their habitual ways of being. (p. viii)

So rather than being answer people, true guides move us away from the habit of believing quick answers are the most ideal steps to living fully. Instead, a guide's response may offer us hope that is wrapped in active patience. In one of the entries from the classic *Letters to a Young Poet*, Ranier Maria Rilke (1954) advises,

> I want to beg you, as much as I can, dear sir, to be patient toward all that is unsolved in your heart and to try to love the questions themselves, like locked rooms and like books that are written in a foreign tongue. Do not now seek the answers, which cannot be given you because you would not be able to live them. And the point is to live everything. Live the questions now. Perhaps you will gradually, without noticing it, live along some distant day into the answers. (pp. 34–35)

MENTORS OF MINDFULNESS ALSO DON'T GET IN THE WAY OF WHAT IS IMPORTANT

No matter how excellent and wise the teacher is, the message or "the Way" (central approach) must remain central. Guides know they can offer much to their apprentices simply by not getting in the way of the lessons the person needs to learn. As Sogyal Rinpoche (1992) notes:

> It cannot be stressed too often that it is the truth of the teaching which is the central focus which is all important, and never the personality of the teacher. This is why Buddha reminded us of the "Four Reliances":
>
> 1. Rely on the message of the teacher, not on his personality;
> 2. Rely on the meaning, not just the words;

3. Rely on the real meaning, not the provisional one;
4. Rely on your wisdom mind, not on your ordinary, judgmental mind. (p. 130)

There is a tendency to put spiritual guides on pedestals and then to be shocked by their clay feet. By recognizing it is "the teaching" or "the Way" in some traditions that must be the ultimate focus, this can be avoided. We must take care in both the selection of our teachers and in looking at the teachings they offer us. As Thomas Merton cautioned, in the search for a full spiritual life we must not be like crows and pick up everything that glitters. Those we see as role models and the teachings we follow must be simultaneously practical and filled with passion. In the end, if the teachings don't change our attitudes and the way we live in a good way, then of what use are they? However, if both the gifts and the teachers are good, then we have an opportunity to embrace and practice what we are taught; this can then lead to a groundbreaking epiphany and a sense of new freedom in our lives. (We must also remember this when others come to us for guidance and care!)

MINDFUL OPENNESS AND EFFORT: GUIDING LIGHTS TO NEW FREEDOM

Being open to the truth with a sense of humility and a recognition that there are so many ways in which we are not free is at the heart of the apprenticeship process. As Sogyal Rinpoche (1992) once again advises:

- View the teacher as physician.
- See oneself as patient.

- Understand teachings as medicine.
- Resolve to follow the teachings for cure. (p. 130)

This is similar to classic desert wisdom. Likewise, it is worthy of embrace now when obedience is rare, and the presence of a true selfless sage is an even more uncommon occurrence. Once again, in a colorful story from the fourth-century desert, the *abbas* were known to say:

If you see a young person climbing to the heavens by his own will, quickly grab him by the foot and pull him right down so he is grounded for what he is doing of his own accord is not good for him. (author's translation)

American Buddhist teacher Jack Kornfield (2000) echoes this theme but with a slightly different emphasis. He notes that awakening depends on:

- Openness of the student
- Earnest willingness to discover
- Significant period of practice (purification)
- Respect and awe surrounding the master
- Field of consciousness of the master—direct presence of love, freedom and emptiness (pp. 80–81)

What Buddhists Sogyal Rinpoche and Jack Kornfield are pointing to is the need to be both open and passionate, simultaneously faithful and hopeful. This emphasis on a faithfulness is unwavering on the part of those seeking help (including many of us) to be doubtful as to whether a guide—or *anyone* for that matter—will really be faithful or of any help to us. This doubt and hesitation can hold us back unless we receive timely encouragement, or in the case of those coming to us, we support them when they shy away from seeking a wisdom figure or following the teachings that will set them free.

Andrew Harvey (1983) reports in his original book, *Journey in Ladakh*, that he shared with a person journeying with him in India, "It is hard to believe in any help." A Tibetan companion wisely responds to this by saying, "That is because you have not found out where the help is" (p. 167). For each of us this person is someone who has a particular gift that will help release us from the inner chains that remain and be able to nourish the seeds of the spiritual life that are presently dormant in us.

THE CHARISM OF THE GUIDE

People have a particular gift or *charism* out of which they live. When we are exposed to this gift we are pulled in by it—for good or bad. Millicent Dillon (1998), in her biography of writer-composer Paul Bowles, with whom she was infatuated, notes:

> Something about Paul, about being with him, made one feel that with him you were at the center of the world—his world, maybe even the world. How this was created, I don't know. But it was obviously felt not only by me but also by those who clustered about him. It was there, palpable in the air. . . . (p. 27)

The guides who have a dramatic effect on us have found a way to share their charism in a very powerful way. If we are to have an equal effect on our apprentices, we must do the same. Jeffrey

Kottler (1986) writes, in his book on being a therapist, that even the philosophy or theory of guiding others is attributable to this underlying personal charism. He notes:

> All effective therapists intuitively find a way to capital-
> ize on the strength of their character. Freud's self-analytic
> skills, Roger's genuineness, Ellis' capacity for rational
> thinking, Perls' playfulness, found the nucleus for their
> respective theories. (n. p.)

PRACTICE, PRACTICE, PRACTICE

Despite the power of their messages and personages, the wisdom figures of old and the contemporary guides noted still indicate that, in the end, much rests with the mentoree, disciple, appren-tice, or student as to how transformative an exposure to such fig-ures and lessons will be. As Sogyal Rinpoche (1992) recognizes, "One of the greatest things to model is being a student all of your life of the great masters." However, he goes on to caution, "You may have the karma (the law of moral effect) to find a teacher, but you must then create the karma to follow your teacher" (p. 132).

This requires more than quick action. Sensitive, intuitive awareness of the spirit and the knowledge of the teaching or teacher is also essential. We must not only appreciate the words of the guides who inspire us, but also listen to the attitude of life flowing behind their words. Anthony de Mello (1986), in speaking of the insightful dialogues he had garnered from many traditions in his book *One Minute Wisdom*, cautioned nonetheless:

> This, alas, is not an easy book! It is written not to
> instruct but to Awaken. Concealed within its pages (not
> in printed words, not even in the tales, but in its spirit,
> its mood, its atmosphere) is Wisdom which cannot be

> conveyed in human speech. . . . That is what Wisdom
> means: To be changed without the slightest effort on your
> part, to be transformed, believe it or not, merely by wak-
> ing to the reality that is not words, that lies beyond the
> reach of words. (pp. 2–3)

This is exactly what true mentors of mindfulness convey to those who interact with them personally. It is what we can expect if we bring the right motivation and effort to our encounters with these ancient and modern wisdom figures, especially if it is not an in-person encounter.

If we are reading their words, we must read, underline, write out what we've underlined, study, think, learn, overlearn, over-over-learn, absorb, practice, and then begin looking at it again as if we were children. The last several points are especially essential—whether it is through reading or actual contact with a sage. We must employ what we have learned. If the teachings are to become deeply rooted, we need to *practice, practice, practice* with those people (client, family, friends, co-workers, acquaintances, and especially those with whom we normally don't get along or who challenge us) who are in front of us every day. We also need to experiment with new behaviors and attitudes learned with strangers who don't have a habitual response to us and can further help us build our new practice.

Such practice, if it is good, will soften our souls. It will make us embrace everything that comes our way so the fruits can be good for us and those with whom we interact. In place of grasping, there will be freedom; in place of confusion, greater clarity and simplic-ity; in place of anxiety, more peace and a greater sense of inner ease. It is not that we will never experience pain, but how we deal with it will be different. No matter how much painful reality comes our way, we will be able to say with confidence, "I really don't have a care in the world." Truly that is the pearl of great price. Seeking this pearl has led to great wisdom, not only in a fourth-century

Egyptian desert or other ancient time, but in other periods and places as well. Different world spiritualities share this quest for inner freedom, and the teachings of all serious seekers are worthy of reflection and practice as a way of making ancient and modern wisdom even more part and parcel of our contemporary lives.

There is, however, one final caution about practice. Often when the practice we are involved in doesn't bring the immediate or exact results we wish, we feel that we have failed. This negative feeling doesn't take into consideration the overall value and positive affect of good spiritual practice designed to rid us of bad habits. Shunryu Suzuki (2002) addresses this well in a reflection on Buddhist practice and his own life that he shared with his students. Because it brings to the fore two essential spiritual themes (practice and humility) to recall and repeatedly meditate on particularly in the deserts of life, it is a fitting one with which to close this chapter.

> My own habit is absentmindedness. I am naturally very forgetful. Even though I started working on it when I went to my teacher at the age of thirteen, I have not been able to do anything about it. It is not because of old age that I am forgetful [now], it is my tendency. But working on it, I found that I could get rid of my selfish way of doing things. If the purpose of practice and training was just to correct your weak points, I think it would be almost impossible to succeed. Even so, it is necessary to work on them, because as you work on them, your character will be trained and you will become free of ego.
>
> People say I am very patient, but actually I have a very impatient character. My inborn character is very impatient. I don't try to correct it any longer, but I don't think my effort was in vain, because I studied many things. I had to be very patient in order to work on my

habit, and I must be very patient when people criticize me about my forgetfulness. "Oh! He is so forgetful, we cannot rely on him at all. What should we do with him?"

My teacher scolded me every day: "This forgetful boy!" But I just wanted to stay with him. I didn't want to leave him. I was very patient with whatever he said. So I think that is why I am very patient with whatever he said. So I think that is why I am patient with others' criticism about me. Whatever they say, I don't mind so much. I am not so angry with them. If you know how important it is to train yourself in this way, I think you will understand. . . . This is the most important point in our practice. (p. 92)

Some Questions to Consider at This Point

> Have you ever been in a mentoring relationship? What were your mentors like?
>
> What would you need to be especially aware of if and when you were in a mentoring role?
>
> If you were to imagine an ideal mentor for you at this point in your life, what would this person be like?
>
> What are the good psychological costs counselors should be willing to bear when they receive mentoring?
>
> What is the most effective way for you to put into practice the essentials you have learned in a mentoring relationship or the wisdom you have received from books, CDs, or presentations/lectures which in some way you felt mentored by?

APPENDIX

——◆——

Retreat and Reflect: Enjoying a Fresh Experience of Your Own Inner Life

One doesn't take a journey into the Himalayas without a guide who knows the ancient paths.

—Jack Kornfield (1995),
A Path with Heart

In the pages that follow, themes that have been discussed in the book (as well as some essential allied ones) are presented in the compelling words of some of the leading thinkers, practitioners, and mentors on how to develop a strong inner life. I have been so moved by their words that I read and reflect on them again and again. To me, the telling point about their significance is that they impel one to *act*, rather than merely admire them from afar.

Although each person's learning and reflective style is unique, taking a few moments with one or two of these quotes each day would seem to maximize their impact. I would suggest not skimming through them, or if for some reason you still prefer to do so, to then return and reread them at a slower pace. I think if you do, you will find the results to be rewarding in terms of enhancing mindfulness and opening up new inner space in which to enjoy your life and help others who seek your counsel to better appreciate theirs.

MENTORS OF ALONETIME
AND READINESS

Jack Kornfield (2000) writes in his book *After the Ecstasy, the Laundry*:

> The understanding of emptiness is contagious: It appears we can catch it from one another. We know that when a sad or angry person enters a room, we too often enter into sadness or anger. It shouldn't surprise us, then, that the presence of a teacher who is empty, open, awake can have a powerful effect on another person, especially if that person is ripe. (p. 79)

To be healthy, counselors who are empty themselves need good friends who are also empty, humble, selfless, open. Who are these people in your life and what is each of them teaching and calling you to be? Also, what can you do to improve your readiness to receive such counsel?

APPRECIATING OUR CENTER OF GRAVITY

To find out what is contaminating our own space, meditation can help, in Brazier's words, by "quieting habitual energies: cleansing perception so we can see what is going on. Mindfulness is an attempt to regain contact with the flow of experience . . . it is not uncommon for people to live their whole lives in front of an imaginary audience" (pp. 73, 96).

What is it that is really holding [our client's] attention? . . . [What is] the centre of gravity around which all [the] client's subliminal attention orbits? (p. 61)
—*David Brazier (1995),* Zen Therapy

He goes on to say at another point in his book that "Therapy is not to get rid of discomfort, but to experience truth, which means that the therapist must be beyond needing to be popular" (p. 209).

In pointing this out, Brazier is raising our awareness to our own center of gravity as we seek to get our clients to be more aware of theirs. What preoccupies us during the day? Before we go to bed? Under states of diminished consciousness (when sick, dreaming, under the influence of alcohol, medication, drugs, anger, anxiety or stress)? Such examination will not only help us see our need to be popular, but it will also help us grasp so much more about ourselves.

SIMPLICITY AND CLARITY

What does "simple living" mean to a counselor? Beyond such things as living within our financial means (which is exterior), what is *inner simplicity* to you? What is the philosophy by which you live, the identity at the core of yourself? What is left if I take away your reputation, name, friends, family, even health? If what remains after that is your essence, what is it?

[The present Dalai Lama] sits in front of the scientists as unselfconsciously as if sitting alone in his room at home . . . [with] acuity and alertness. . . . But the Dalai Lama impresses, or disarms, me by doing away with many of the categories with which we imprison ourselves. . . . It's the questions he puts into play that invigorate . . . and he really does aspire, as every monk does, to a simplicity that lies not before complexity but on the far side of it, having not dodged experience but subsumed it. . . . At times he pulls out a piece of tissue from his shoulder bag and polishes his glasses—which might, I realize, be a metaphor for what he's encouraging all of us to do. (pp. 13, 15, 16, 19, 23)

—*Pico Iyer* (2008), The Open Road

A POSITIVE ANTISOCIAL ACT

Society has long had problems with people spending time in silence and solitude. As author Anne Morrow Lindbergh (1955) remarks in her book *Gift from the Sea*:

> If one sets aside time for a business appointment, a trip to the hairdresser, a social engagement, or a shopping expedition, that time is accepted as inviolable. But if one says: I cannot come because that is my hour to be alone, one is considered rude, egotistical or strange. (p. 50)

How do you build silence, solitude, and mindfulness meditation into your own schedule and life as you would a client appointment, time for a meal, exercise, or a phone call, a visit to a relative, and the hours when you sleep?

BALANCE

Edwin Storr quite aptly notes,

> The burden of value with which we are at present loading interpersonal relationships is too heavy for those fragile craft to carry. . . . [L]ove and friendship are, of course, an important part of what makes life worthwhile. But they are not the only source of happiness. (Quoted in Maitland, 2008, p. 134)

As counselors, much discipline is required of us during sessions so we are able to reflect rather than react to the client. Given this, there must also be spaces of freedom, reflection, and renewal in our own life if this is to remain possible in an ongoing way in our practice and our life beyond the clinical hours. How do you now balance encounter with one of the other main sources of silence: *alonetime*? Given the importance of these periods of time by and with yourself, how do you plan on expanding them in a realistic way that you can and will act upon?

DISCOVERING SILENT SPACES

In Maitland's (2008) *A Book of Silence*, she remarks that,

> Silence, even as an expression of awe, is becoming uncomfortable. We are asked to be silent less and less; churches and public libraries are no longer regarded as places where silence is appropriate . . . silence is not experienced as refreshing or as assisting concentration, but as threatening and disturbing. . . . Nonetheless, despite the rising tide of noise, there are some real pools of silence embedded in the noisiest places and I began to search them out. (pp. 137–138)

Finding silence, and possibly a measure of solitude, isn't simply finding a place in your own schedule when you have time. It is also finding an actual physical place where you can be on your own. Where are these places for you? How and when do you access them? Is there a certain place that is especially welcoming for longer periods of silence and mindfulness meditation? Is there a ritual of quiet renewal that is a daily experience of your own presence, breathing, and not being in a cognitive cocoon that prevents you from experiencing the moment?

FINDING THE CENTRAL PRINCIPLE

Once again, in Pico Iyer's (2008) book on the Dalai Lama, *The Open Road*, he writes:

> Monks tend to be sparing with their words, precise-few "um's" and "er's"—because they have cut away everything that is inessential and their words emerge from an abundant silence. Often the Dalai Lama will say nothing for what seems like minutes after I ask him something, and I can almost see him gathering himself and sorting through his mind to find the central principal [sic]. (p. 153)

In place of being intellectually quick or glib, which is usually valued by the culture at large, do you seek to be centered, clear, and transparent when you respond? What would help you take the space so this style would increase? What would release you from image, the need to be right, or to control the situation? What would keep you from interacting out of a desire to be seen as bright, attractive, or special that would then allow you to interact freely and openly so those in your presence could be released from their ego prisons as well?

TRANSPARENCY

In *Bones of the Master*, George Crane (2000) writes about Tsung Tsai, a Chan Master. In the following passage, he is observing him and a fellow Chinese Buddhist:

> *Two old men*, I thought. *Simple as uncarved wood.* They had none of my guilt and anger; none of my arrogance

or sarcasm. There was a calmness about them, a startling sense of completion. They were, it seemed, without yearning, something unimaginable in men. They embodied Zen: *Be happy to live. Be happy to die. Do your work and pass on.*

They were beyond my fear that the universe was without meaning, beyond my grasping for understanding, for the Buddha always just out of reach. I thought about confessing, telling them all the awful things I had done. My deceits or cheats, as Tsung Tsai would have called them. *Cheat who?* Tsung Tsai would have asked. *Everybody, Tsung Tsai. Everybody.* When I looked up, they were staring at me with dark, wet eyes.

"Georgie, Georgie," Tsung Tsai sighed. "You so sad. Sometimes so foolish. So much worry. Your fox mind." (p. 277)

What do our worries and preoccupations teach us about ourselves? What do we need to release? What prevents us from being persons without guile who are then able to purify the psychological and spiritual air for others? What reflective, mindful, meditative practice or mentorship would also help us in this regard?

A PERSON WITHOUT GUILE

In another passage from *Bones of the Master*, Crane (2000) writes about a visit to China in which he accompanied his friend Tsung Tsai, who wished to return to the site of his monastery, which was torn down by the Red Guard, who also forced him to flee.

We picked our way across the field. The ground was barren, charred with salt. . . . Tsung Tsai stumbled in broken footfalls. I took his arm, but he shook me off. We came to a tree, and he leaned against it, occasionally wiping his eyes with the back of his hand. Over his shoulder, I watched a man appear like a mirage from behind a rise, leading a donkey loaded with cane. He stopped when he saw us, took off his cap, and clawed his fingers through his hair. Then he hurried forward, going straight up to Tsung Tsai and prostrating himself. Tsung Tsai helped him to his feet.

"Wang Guey Ru," Tsung Tsai said. "My old friend. Also a very good Buddhist."

Good Buddhist, I thought ruefully, was how Tsung Tsai described everyone. If you weren't Attila the Hun you were a good Buddhist. (p. 143)

What allows us to embrace the goodness of humanity and not just its negative side? How do we embrace mindfulness so we can replace the anger, harsh judgment, rejection, resentment, hurt, self-debasement, and other dark feelings and cognitions that rise so spontaneously in us with other positive emotions and realities?

On the Internet and television news shows there seems to be an underlying belief that the negative is more real than the positive. How do we stop swallowing this in the culture and in ourselves by catching when this happens and reorienting ourselves by assertively disputing and balancing it? Isn't this one of the thrusts of the positive psychology movement today that doesn't dispute individual and societal problems but says there is more to the human being—i.e., the person's "signature strengths"—and society (positive aspects of institutions that call us to experience life more fully) than simply a person and a community in need of repair?

LIFE AS A PILGRIMAGE

What would need to happen to transform your life from simply being a bundle of trivial practical chores that must be done each day at your clinical practice and at home into a pilgrimage so you could see yourself not just as a clinician or in other roles but instead as a mindful companion to your clients, family, friends, others, and yourself? What rituals would you need to put into place to confer your life with a new kind of dignity and change it into a true pilgrimage that would actually affect your style of daily living *immediately*?

> By naming my journey a pilgrimage, he had conferred a kind of dignity on it that altered the way I have traveled ever since. . . . [T]here is something sacred waiting to be discovered in virtually every journey . . . a journey of risk and renewal. For a journey without challenge has no meaning; one without purpose has no soul. (p. xx)
> —*Phil Cousineau (1998)*,
> The Art of Pilgrimage

A QUIET WALK

As counselors, we know that activity and

> Above all, do not lose your desire to walk: Every day I walk myself into a state of well-being and walk away from every illness; I have walked myself into my best thoughts. (quoted in Cousineau, 1998, p. 25)
> —*Soren Kierkegaard, philosopher*

depression do not like to live together. We also can appreciate
the poor oxygen exchange in many of the buildings in which
we work. Exercise can help raise our spirits, but we have many
reasons (excuses?) not to do it. However, we can always take
out time for a short walk. Walking is a cornerstone of physical and mental health; it is an opportunity to enjoy being with
yourself.

PERSPECTIVE AND INTRIGUE

Frontiersman Daniel Boone's
reply when asked if he had ever
been lost: "No. But I was
bewildered once for three days."
(p. 156)

—*Phil Cousineau (1988)*,
The Art of Pilgrimage

As we now know from the
research on posttraumatic
growth, it is not the size
of the trauma as much as
the person's perception
and type of reaction to it
that determines its effect as
well as the rate of recovery
and depth of the insight
gained. Both spiritual-
ity and psychology appreciate that our mind can make a hell of
heaven and a heaven of hell. Instead of getting lost in the three
psychological *cul de sacs* of arrogance (projection), ignorance
(condemning self), and discouragement (wanting the world to
conform to our "needs" now), when perspective is valued a spirit
of *intrigue* about our own reactions and the world we live in are
present. Our frozen schemas can then be melted, and we can
experience life more directly and not grasp onto what will hold
us fast from being open and able to let go so we can change as
life changes.

DEVELOPING YOUR OWN CULTURE OF SILENCE

How can more silence, little by little, be introduced into the car, home, office, our places of walking and exercising? How can we silence our mind so we are able to go for a walk instead of "going for a think"? Those are some of the questions facing us—especially as counselors—today in our noisy, intense, combustible culture.

I think silence is one of these things that has unfortunately been dropped from our culture. We don't have a culture of silence. . . . Young Romans or young Greeks were taught to keep silent in very different ways according to the people with whom they were interacting. Silence was then a specific form of experiencing a relationship with others. This is something that I believe is really worth cultivating. I'm in favor of developing silence as an inner and outer cultural ethos. (pp. 3–4)

—*Michel Foucault (1988),*
Politics, Philosophy, and Culture

STILLNESS, IMPERMANENCE, AND AWE

In his book, *First You Have to Row a Little Boat*, Richard Bode (1993) muses:

I once met a man who said he had visited every exotic place from the Grand Canyon to the Great Wall, but when I questioned him closely I discovered he hadn't seen the songbirds in his own backyard.

What I would like to suggest to such people is that they sit perfectly still and stare intently into a lily pond. But that's difficult advice to give and even more difficult to accept in a society that holds contemplation in such low self-esteem. . . . Must we die and come back to our tiny place on Planet Earth, as Emily comes back in Thornton Wilder's *Our Town*, to experience the snail's pace of love. There's no cry in our literature more poignant, more anguished than Emily's in that terrible moment before she returns to her grave on the hill.

"Good-by, good-by, world. Good-by, Grover's Corners . . . Mama and Papa. Good-by to clocks ticking . . . and Mama's sunflowers. And food and coffee. And new-ironed dresses and hot baths . . . and sleeping and waking up. Oh, earth, you're too wonderful for anybody to realize you. (She looks toward the stage manager and asks abruptly, through her tears.) Do any human beings ever realize life while they live it?—every, every minute?"

And the stage manager replies, "No. The saints and poets, maybe—they do some." (p. 134)

The passage from *Our Town* is so poignant that a comment by me to spur reflection is unnecessary. What does it stir in you?

FACING OUR MATERIALISM

As counselors work with their clients on *quality* of life, it should not be surprising that a charlatanism sometimes rears its head as the counselors themselves are preoccupied in their own lives with the *quantity* of life. How might we reframe our lives in ways where we are not spending so much of our resources (personal and financial) on what we don't really need materially to be happy, on expending concern on such events as client cancellations or bad weather preventing us from seeing clients (and earning the money)? What do we need to do to have at least as much discipline and awareness in this area as we expect our clients to have or gain?

Thoreau encourages us, when buying things, to think of their labor cost—that is, the amount of life we have to give up to obtain money to buy the thing in question. . . . If we simplify our lives, it won't require much labor to earn our living . . . and leave us free for more important endeavors, such as being the self-appointed and unpaid inspector of snowstorms and rainstorms. (p. 262)
                          —*Sara Maitland (2008),*
                          The Book of Silence

HONORING A SABBATH IN OUR LIVES

As De Quincey recognized,

> No man ever will unfold the capacities of his intellect who does not at least checker his life with solitude.

My oldest brother Ron was asked shortly after retiring, "What's it like?" "Oh, wonderful," he responded. Then, with an expression of dismay, he noted, "But Fridays are not as much fun or as meaningful to me anymore." His week ran at one speed. No longer did he have the anticipation of a Sabbath that was pronounced with a different rhythm. Most people today who are not retired have a similar experience but for a different reason: Friday means little because the weekends are not any different than the rest of the week. This is potentially dangerous, not only physically, as we saw during World War II when people worked nonstop and became less, rather than more productive. It also may cause, as De Quincey noted, quite adverse reactions to our potential. Where is the Sabbath in a week and a life? Where is the solitude that allows us to be released so we don't race to our grave but savor our life? Where?

UNPLEASANT SURFACINGS ON THE ROAD TO GREATER FREEDOM

In his book on desert wisdom, Henri Nouwen (1981) writes:

> In solitude I get rid of my scaffolding: no friends to talk with, no telephone calls to make, no meetings to attend, no music to entertain, no books to distract, just me—naked, vulnerable, weak, sinful, deprived, broken— nothing. It is this nothingness that I have to face in solitude, a nothingness so dreadful that everything in me wants to run to my friends, my work, and my distractions so that I can forget my nothingness and make myself believe that I am worth something. But that is not all. As soon as I decide to stay in my solitude, confusing ideas, disturbing images, wild fantasies, and weird associations jump in my mind. (p. 27)

Silence and solitude are not rare in life because we are too busy but because when we take it, initially we may be disturbed. Yet, being with that negative music playing allows it to rise up and leave our preconscious to give us the space to understand, address, and maybe even laugh at it all rather than have it rumbling below the surface during the day, without our awareness.

DIFFERING VIEWS OF SOLITUDE

Henri Nouwen (1981), once again from his book *Way of the Heart*, on alonetime:

> [W]e think of solitude as a place where we gather new strength to continue the ongoing competition in life. . . . But that is not the solitude of [other well-known solitaries]. . . . For them solitude is not a private therapeutic place. Rather, it is a place of conversion, the place where the old self dies and the new self is born, the place where the emergencies of the new man and the new woman occurs. (p. 27)

In solitude new doors can open for us. How we face what we see when this happens is very much like grappling with a *koan* (life puzzle): There are no right or wrong answers but responses we decide upon that will start us on a particular road that may change our lives. In the words of a counselor reflecting on her youth, "I let go and hoped I would surface, but where I would surface, I had no idea." One of the exciting surfacings that has often been reported as a result of time in silence and solitude is the finding of one's own voice. This can happen even to seasoned counselors *if* they allow themselves to remain beginners and let it.

ALONETIME AS AN OPPORTUNITY TO RELEASE OURSELVES FROM COMPARISON

In his book, *On Desire: Why We Want What We Want*, William B. Irvine (2006) confronts us with the following reflections and question:

Because fame requires the cooperation of other people, it puts us at the mercy of those same people. . . . How would our behavior change if other people vanished? It is only a slight exaggeration to say we live for other people—that the bulk of our time, energy, and wealth is spent creating and maintaining a certain public image of ourselves. . . . Soren Kierkegaard characterizes envy as failed admiration because the feelings are mixed with a sense of injustice. (pp. 36, 41, 44)

How much energy would we save if unproductive comparisons were not part of our center of gravity? How much energy would then be available for us and those we co-journey with to simply enjoy life if comparisons were less and flowing with our life was more of a reality? When we catch ourselves making comparisons with other people, counselors, professions, or in other ways, this is an ideal time to explore our sense of dissatisfaction or feelings of triumphs.

LOVING FAMILIAR PLACES OF SOLITUDE WITHIN

Thomas Merton once wrote,

Solitude is not found so much by looking outside the boundaries of your dwelling as by staying within. Solitude is not something to hope for in the future. Rather it is a deepening of the present and unless you look for it in the present you will never find it. (source unknown)

Where is this quiet place within where we can rest and welcome thoughts, feelings, experiences, and people who are suffering? How can we enhance our encounter with alonetime so our time in silence and possibly solitude is not flat but rich and renewing? What and how are our readings on mindfulness or encounters with a mentor helping this to be so?

RELISHING PRIVATE SPACE

What are ways we can lean back from our intense interpersonal world so we can breathe and think, relax and observe the world without judgment but with open, observing, receptive senses?

GENTLENESS, A SENSE OF HUMOR, AND BEING IN THE NOW

Gentleness and a sense of humor are human traits that can make life better for those we encounter. They even go farther, in their positive effect, I think, when we turn them on ourselves. In the serious business of counseling, they help us to become

The phrase "personal space" had a quaint, seventies ring to it ("You're invading my space, man"), but it is one of those gratifying expressions that is intuitively understood by all human beings. Like the twelve-mile limit around our national shores, personal space is our individual border beyond which no stranger can penetrate without making us uneasy. Lately, I've found that my personal space is being violated more than ever before. (p. 90)
—*Richard Stengel (1995),*
The New Yorker

We really don't want to stay with the nakedness of our present experience. It goes against the grain to stay present. There are times when only gentleness and a sense of humor can give us the strength to settle down.
—*Pema Chodron (1997),*
When Things Fall Apart

and remain more psychologically supple and receptive to new perspectives. What would represent for you "red flags of emotion" in your practice and life that would incur the need for such gentle treatment of and by yourself? When do you tease yourself in a nice way? What other areas in your life does humor and gentle self-discussion need to take place?

SIMPLICITY AND MEANING-MAKING

There was an old psychodynamic axiom that, *As a counselor you can't take a client any further than you have gone yourself.* Whether this is absolutely true or not, it points to the need for clarity, self-awareness, maturity, and compassion in the counselor. Probably there is no faster route to achieving this than having a sense of simplicity and possessing a sensitivity to meaning-making. Simplicity is one of the leading ways to prevent our ego from deluding us. Honoring how we make meaning allows us to avoid being swayed by values that are built on defensiveness, competition, comparisons, and an ethos in society that is centered on the wrong things with respect to happiness (e.g., financial wealth, fame, possessions). How do simplicity and meaning-making evidence themselves in your life as a counselor and a person?

Simplifying one's life to extract its quintessence is the most rewarding of all the pursuits I have undertaken. It doesn't mean giving up what is truly beneficial, but finding out what really matters and what brings lasting fulfillment, joy, serenity, and above all, the irreplaceable boon of altruistic love. It means transforming oneself to better transform the world. (p. 14)
—*Matthieu Richard (2003)*,
Happiness

SOLITUDE'S RENEWAL

In *Man's Search for Meaning*, Viktor Frankl, who spent three harrowing years in the Nazi concentration camp, Auschwitz, found it absolutely essential to find crumbs of alonetime. With his powerful lesson before us, how and when do we take these periods of space in our own life, which is so much more fortunate than his life was during this dire period? How can we be inspired by him to value one of the primary conduits to not merely survive but thrive in a life that is so short?

The prisoner craved to be alone with himself and his thoughts. He yearned for privacy and solitude. After my transportation to a so-called "rest camp" I had the rare fortune to find solitude for about five minutes at a time. Behind the earthen hut where I worked and in which were crowded about fifty delirious patients, there was a quiet spot in a corner of the double fence of barbed wire surrounding the camp. A tent had been improvised there with a few poles and branches of trees in order to shelter a half-dozen corpses (the daily death rate in the camp). There was also a shaft leading to the water pipes. I squatted on the wooden lid of this shaft whenever my services were not needed. I just sat and looked out at the green flowering slopes and the distant blue hills of the Bavarian landscape, framed by the meshes of barbed wire. I dreamed longingly, and my thoughts wandered north and northeast, in the direction of my home, but I could only see clouds. . . . The corpses near me, crawling with lice, did not bother me. Only the steps of passing guards could rouse me from my dreams. (p. 81)

—*Viktor Frankl (1968)*,
Man's Search for Meaning

QUIET RECOGNITION AND NEW COMMITMENT

One of the obvious reasons we do not take time alone is that when we clear out our consciousness we create a vacuum into which can arise memories, denials, avoidances, past burdens, and the recognition that we have distanced ourselves from the truth in so many ways. Yet, as a counselor you know that the only memory or silently held belief that can hurt you is the one not remembered and engaged in a healthy fashion. Lives can be led in unnecessary ways and move in directions—even apparently good ones—when the total truth is not surfaced. Also, once we recognize our limitations clearly, the opportunity for almost unlimited growth and development are almost limitless.

For a good part of each day, particularly when [my dog] Logos and I were walking, most particularly when I stopped to sit on a certain log that had been washed up on the sand, I compelled myself to become aware. . . . And one day I came upon the purpose I had been pursuing all the preceding years. I had not known I had been doing that thing: I had believed I had been doing something quite different. So it was a huge thing to learn. Understandable, but ugly. Not palatable in any way. . . . When the thing I had been concealing from myself emerged, I raged, screamed, I wept. After a time I said, "So that's how it is." Not too much later I said, "No longer." (pp. 2, 8)

—*Alice Koller (1990)*,
The Stations of Solitude

SOLITUDE AND COMMUNITY

How have you noticed the interplay of solitude and community in your own life? What ways do you determine when it is out of balance in one way or the other, given your own personality, needs, and life-giving style of living during the day, week, month, and year?

Solitude is essential to community life because in solitude we grow closer to each other. . . . We take the other with us into solitude and there the relationship grows and depends. In solitude we discover each other in a way which physical presence makes difficult, if not possible. There we recognize a bond with each other that does not depend on words, gestures or actions and that is deeper and stronger than our own efforts can create. (p. 18)

—*Henri Nouwen (1978),*
Worship

RESPECTING YOUR PLACES OF SOLITUDE

What are the *different* actual places where you avail yourself of solitude? Which places suit which moods for you?

The sea did [the poet, Rilke] good; "it cleanses me with its noise and lays a rhythm upon everything in me that is disturbed and confused." When at times to his surprise, it seemed not so beneficial, "too loud and too incessant," he would withdraw into the woods where he had found a great reclining tree root on which he "sat for hours as alone on the first day of the world." Chronicled in Rilke's *Letters to a Young Poet* (1934; revised edition, 1954, p. 98)

—*Commentary by*
M. D. Herter Norton

OUR SPACE IS THEIR SPACE

When the tide rises, the boats
also rise.

—*Chinese proverb*

How *deeply* are you aware of the fact that your perceptions, moods, cognitions, and inner space affect others? Please recall and write down illustrations that bear this out so you may return to what you have written later in the day or week so you may reflect further on your illustrations.

SOLITUDE: THE CHALLENGE AND THE GIFT

Maybe I was slowly becoming a prisoner of people's expectations instead of a man liberated by divine promises. Maybe . . . It was not all that clear, but I realized that I would only know by stepping back and allowing the hard questions to touch me even if they hurt. But stepping back was not so easy. I had succeeded in surrounding myself with so many classes to prepare, lectures to give, articles to finish, people to meet, phone calls to make, and letters to answer, that I had come quite close to believing I was indispensible.

What are the hypocrisies and hopes you have with respect to uncovering and availing yourself of silence and solitude? Will you treat yourself to a period of time (an hour possibly?) when you can sit, breathe, and reflect on this essential question?

When I took a closer look at this I realized that I was caught in a web of strange paradoxes. While complaining about too many demands, I felt uneasy when none were made. While speaking about the burden of letter writing, an empty mailbox made me sad. While fretting about tiring lecture tours, I felt disappointed when there were no invitations. While speaking nostalgically about an empty desk, I feared the day on which that would come true. In short: while desiring to be alone, I was frightened of being left alone. The more I became aware of these paradoxes, the more I started to see how much I had indeed fallen in love with my own compulsions and illusions, and how much I needed to step back and wonder, "Is there a quiet stream underneath the fluctuating affirmations and rejections of my little world? Is there a still point where my life is anchored and from which I can reach out with hope and courage and confidence?" (pp. 13–14)

—*Henri Nouwen (1976)*,
The Genesee Diary

MELTING THE EGO

"I wish to become a teacher of the truth."

"Are you prepared to be ridiculed, ignored and starving till you are forty-five?"

"I am. But tell me: What will happen after I am forty-five?"

"You will have grown accustom to it." (p. 19)

The Master seemed quite impervious to what people thought of him. When the disciples asked how he had attained this stage of freedom, he laughed aloud and said, "Till I was twenty I did not care what people thought of me. After twenty I worried endlessly about what my neighbors thought. Then one day after fifty I suddenly saw that they never thought of me at all." (p. 91)
—*Anthony deMello*,
One Minute Wisdom

How often in your clinical practice and other daily encounters do you find yourself concerned with what people think or trying to positively emphasize your own ego by trying to impress others? When you do this, if you can't control doing it, are you able to at least recognize that this is going on in you and figure out what is prompting such self-protection and inflation?

A Brief Final Comment on a Counselor's Inner Renewal in Alonetime

Counseling, to be true to its mission, to have real power, must be countercultural; namely, we must believe that (1) true wealth is inner freedom, not freedom to choose among the many offerings society has sold to us as being indispensible for our happiness; and (2) true power is based on uncovering our own ignorance and being able to unlearn, not being more aware of others' weaknesses so we can take advantage of them.

In the following dialogue between Abbot and psychiatrist John Eudes Bamburger and psychologist and spiritual writer Henri Nouwen, we can see the primary driving force of the previous reflective questions you have reviewed in the Appendix and in this book as a whole—essentially, the need to lean back from our emotions and unexamined unrealistic thoughts, be mindful, shake yourself free from what is preoccupying you and directing you in an unproductive direction, and experience greater inner space that can then be shared with your clients and others.

Here is Nouwen (1976) reflecting on his interactions with Bamburger, his mentor:

> We talked for a moment about torture and brainwashing, and John Eudes told me that in his psychiatric practice he had met a man who, as prisoner of war, underwent much torture but never gave an inch. He was a very simple, down-to-earth man with little political or ideological sophistication. But no pressure was able to force him

to any kind of confession. John Eudes explained this by pointing to the man's sense of identity. No self-doubt, no insecurities, no false guilt feelings that could be exploited by his enemies.

How to come to this simplicity, this inner sense of self, this conviction of self-worth? "Meditate," John Eudes said, "and explore the small daily events in which you can see your insecurity at work. By meditation you can create distance, and what you can keep at a distance, you can shake off" (p. 181).

My hope for you is that you will commit yourself to do likewise.

About the Author

Robert J. Wicks, who received his doctorate in psychology from Hahnemann Medical College and Hospital, is a professor at Loyola University Maryland, where he teaches in the largest CACREP-approved counseling program of its type in the world. He has also served on the faculty of Bryn Mawr College's Graduate School for Social Work and Social Research and taught in professional schools of medicine, nursing, and clinical psychology. He is author of *The Resilient Clinician* (Oxford, 2008), the best-selling *Riding the Dragon* (Sorin Books, 2003), and co-author of *Primer on Posttraumatic Growth* (Wiley, 2012).

In 1994, Dr. Wicks was responsible for the psychological debriefing of relief workers evacuated from Rwanda during that country's bloody civil war. He worked in Cambodia in both 1993 and 2001 with English-speaking helpers from around the world who were helping to rebuild the country after years of terror and torture. In 2006, he also delivered presentations on self-care at the National Naval Medical Center and Walter Reed Army Hospital to those behavioral and health care professionals responsible for treating Iraqi and Afghani war veterans who were evacuated to the United States with multiple amputations and severe head injuries. Dr. Wicks has received the Humanitarian of the Year Award from the American Counseling Association's Division on Spirituality, Ethics, and Values. In 2006, he also was the recipient of the first annual Alumni Award for Excellence in Professional Psychology from Widener University.

RELATED BOOKS BY ROBERT J. WICKS

Primer on Posttraumatic Growth. (2012). Hoboken, NJ: Wiley. (Written with Mary Beth Werdel)

Streams of Contentment. (2011). Notre Dame, IN: Sorin Books.

The Resilient Clinician. (2008) New York, NY: Oxford University Press.

Riding the Dragon. (2003). Notre Dame, IN: Sorin Books.

Recommended Readings

Zen Therapy by David Brazier is one of the finest books I have ever read on both therapy and the therapist—after all, how can they be separated? It is, to my mind, a true contemporary classic on the process of therapy. Other books in this genre include Epstein's *Psychotherapy without the Self* and the work he is especially known for, *Thoughts without a Thinker*, as well as Mruk and Hartzell's *Zen and Psychotherapy* and Bien's *The Zen of Helping*. I think you will also find very useful the edited volume *Mindfulness and Psychotherapy* by Germer, Siegel, and Fulton.

Jeffrey Kottler's work *On Being a Therapist* is the best all-around treatment of the challenges and joys of being a clinician. His other books amplify on the themes he treats in this fine book.

Jack Kornfield is both a psychologist and Zen Master. Of all the books on contemporary Buddhism and how its tenets relate to living a healthy life, no matter what your spirituality or philosophy, I found his works the most helpful, especially *The Wise Heart*, *A Path with Heart* and *After the Ecstasy, the Laundry*. A good accompanying volume to Kornfield's work is Germer's *The Mindful Path to Self-Compassion* and Matthieu Ricard's book *Happiness*.

A psychologist and Christian spiritual writer, Henri Nouwen's book *Reaching Out* is a gem. It is probably his most classic work on the balance between compassion and self-care, understanding, and love. He also co-authored (with Morrison and McNeill) a book on *Compassion*, which counselors from a Christian background would find of real interest. His book on desert wisdom, *Way of the Heart*, is also an excellent treatment of the topic of silence and solitude. A good companion to this last book is Thomas Merton's *Way of the Desert* and *New Seeds of Contemplation*, as well as David Steindl-Rast's beautifully written book *Gratefulness, the Heart of Prayer*.

When Things Fall Apart by Pema Chodron is also written from a Buddhist perspective but is of interest to a wider audience. Again, I think it will be helpful to counselors' own lives as well as in redefining the treatment process they undertake. Another Eastern work is by Sogyal Rinpoche, entitled *Glimpse After Glimpse*, which offers quotes from his longer work, *The Tibetan Book of Living and Dying*.

Anthony deMello, who seeks to combine the psychological insights of both East and West is also worth reading and reflecting upon. His meshing of cognitive psychology, transactional analysis, and Buddhist/Hindu/Christian thinking is very helpful in approaching both mindfulness and life. *One Minute Wisdom*, *A Way to Love*, *Awareness*, and *Sadhana* are good places to start in reading his work.

A re-read of Viktor Frankl's *Will to Meaning*, Etty Hillesum's *An Interrupted Life*, and Rilke's *Letters to a Young Poet* would help a counselor regain both personal and professional perspective in tough times. Perspective is so elusive. There is a Spanish proverb that goes, "I complained that I had no shoes until I met a man who had no feet." Yet, after walking a few more steps, we often quietly quip in ways that miss our attention, "But I still have no shoes!"

The best-researched volume on the theme of alonetime is Philip Koch's *Solitude: A Philosophical Encounter*. I found in it innumerable sources that were a great help in preparing sections of this book. Other key books on silence and solitude include Anthony Storr's *Solitude* and Sara Maitland's *A Book of Silence*.

Jewish works by Abraham Twerski and Aryeh Kaplan and a volume that includes a collection of quotes from the books of Abraham Joshua Heschel, entitled *I Asked for Wonder*, are also worth reviewing for their many insightful reflections and the guidance they offer.

Additional books in the areas of clinician self-care, secondary stress, resiliency, mindfulness, and positive psychology are included in the general Bibliography.

References

Albom, M. (1997). *Tuesdays with Morrie: An old man, a young man, and life's greatest lesson.* New York, NY: Doubleday.

An interview with Thich Nhat Hanh, Vietnamese Zen master (1989). *Common Boundary,* Nov./Dec., 16.

Armstrong, K. (2000). *Buddha.* New York, NY: Penguin.

Bloom, A. (1970). *Beginning to pray.* Mahwah, NJ: Paulist Press.

Bode, R. (1993). *First you have to row a little boat.* New York, NY: Warner.

Braza, J. (1997). *Moment by moment: The art and practice of mindfulness.* New Clarendon, VT: Tuttle.

Brazier, D. (1995). *Zen therapy: Transcending the sorrows of the human mind.* New York, NY: Wiley.

Buchholz, E. (1997). *The call of solitude: Alonetime in a world of attachment.* New York, NY: Simon & Schuster.

Byrd, R. E. (1938). *Alone: The classic Polar adventure.* London, UK: Putnam.

Chadwick, D. (1999). *The crooked cucumber: The life and Zen teaching of Shunryu Suzuki.* New York, NY: Broadway.

Chadwick, D. (2001). *To shine one corner of the world: Moments with Shunryu Suzuki.* New York, NY: Broadway.

Chodron, P. (1997). *When things fall apart: Heart advice for difficult times.* Boston, MA: Shambala.

Cousineau, P. (1998). *The art of pilgrimage: The seeker's guide to making travel sacred.* Berkeley, CA: Conari Press.

Crane, G. (2000). *Bones of the master: A journey to secret Mongolia.* New York, NY: Bantam.

Csikszentmihalyi, M. (1990). *Flow: The psychology of optimal experience.* New York, NY: Harper.

deMello, A. (1986). *One minute wisdom.* New York, NY: Doubleday.

Dillard, A. (1989). *The writing life.* New York, NY: Harper Collins.

Dillon, M. (1998). *You are not I: A portrait of Paul Bowles.* Berkeley: University of California Press.

Dixon, T. (1999). *The crooked cucumber*. New York, NY: Broadway Books.

du Boulay, S. (1998). *Beyond the darkness: A biography of Bede Griffiths*. New York, NY: Doubleday.

Fischer, N. (2001). Quoted in Henry, P. (Ed.), *Benedict's dharma*. New York, NY: Riverhead.

Foucault, M. (1988). *Politics, philosophy and culture: Interviews and other writing, 1977–1984*. A. Sheridan (Trans.), L. Kritzman (Ed.). New York, NY: Routledge.

France, P. (1996). *Hermits: The insights of solitude*. New York, NY: St. Martin's Press.

Frankl, V. (1968) *Man's search for meaning*. New York, NY: Washington Square Press.

Fredrickson, B. (2002). Positive emotion. In C. R. Snyder & S. J. Lopez (Eds.), *Handbook of positive psychology* (pp. 120–134). New York, NY: Oxford University Press.

Germer, C. K., Siegel, R. D., & Fulton, P. R. (2005). *Mindfulness and psychotherapy*. New York, NY: Guilford Press.

Gregoriou, S. (2000). *Way of the dreamcatcher: Spirit lessons with Robert Lax*. Toronto, Canada: Novalis.

Grumbach, D. (1994). *Fifty days of solitude*. Boston, MA: Beacon Press.

Harvey, A. (1983). *A journey in Ladakh: Encounters with Buddhism*. Boston, MA: Houghton-Mifflin.

Hauser, R. (2000). The minister and personal prayer. In R. Wicks (Ed.), *Handbook of spirituality for ministers* (Vol. 2). Mahwah, NJ: Paulist Press.

Henry, P. (Ed) (2002). Benedict's dharma. New York, NY: Riverhead.

Heschel, A. J. (1951). *The Sabbath: Its meaning for modern man*. New York, NY: Farrar, Straus and Giroux.

Irvine, W. (2006). *On desire: Why we want what we want*. New York, NY: Oxford University Press.

Iyer, P. (2008). *The open road: The global journey of the fourteenth Dalai Lama*. New York, NY: Knopf.

Johnson, S. (1996). *The book of Tibetan elders: The life stories and wisdom of the great spiritual masters of Tibet*. New York, NY: Riverhead.

Kabat-Zinn, J. (1994). *Wherever you go, there you are*. New York, NY: Hyperion.

Kafka, F. (1974). *Letters to Felice*. J. Stern & E. Duckworth (Trans.). New York, NY: Penguin.

Kaplan, A. (1982). *Meditation and the Kabbalah*. York Beach, ME: Samuel Weiser.

Koller, A. (1990). *The stations of solitude*. New York, NY: William Morrow.

Kornfield, J. (1995). *A path with heart: A guide through the perils and promises of spiritual life*. New York, NY: Bantam.

Kornfield, J. (2000). *After the ecstasy, the laundry: How the heart grows wise on the spiritual path*. New York, NY: Bantam.

Kottler, J. (1986/2010). *On being a therapist*. San Francisco, CA: Jossey-Bass.

Leech, K. (1985). *Experiencing God: Theology as spirituality*. San Francisco, CA: Harper.

Maitland, S. (2008). *A book of silence*. Berkeley, CA: Counterpoint.

Matthiessen, P. (1986). *Nine-headed Dragon River*. Boston, MA: Shambala Press.

Merton, T. (1960). *The wisdom of the desert*. New York, NY: New Directions.

Merton, T. (1965). *The way of Chuang Tzu*. New York, NY: New Directions.

Merton, T. (1988). *A vow of conversation: Journals, 1964–1965*. New York, NY: Farrar, Straus and Giroux.

Morrow Lindbergh, A. (1955). *Gift from the sea*. New York, NY: Pantheon.

Norris, K. (1993). *Dakota: A spiritual geography*. Boston, MA: Houghton-Mifflin.

Nouwen, H. (1975). *Reaching out: The three movements of the spiritual life*. New York, NY: Doubleday.

Nouwen, H. (1976). *The Genesee diary: Report from a Trappist Monastery*. New York, NY: Doubleday.

Nouwen, H. (1978). Solitude and community. *Worship*, 52, 15–29.

Nouwen, H. (1981). *The way of the heart: The spirituality of the desert fathers and mothers*. New York, NY: Seabury/Harper.

Percy, W. (1980). *The second coming: A novel*. New York, NY: Picador.

Peterson, C. (2006). *A primer in positive psychology*. New York, NY: Oxford University Press.

Powell, B. (1985). *Alone, alive and well: How to fight loneliness and win*. Rodale, PA: Rodale Press.

Prochnik, G. (2010). *In pursuit of silence: Listening for meaning in a world full of noise*. New York, NY: Doubleday.

Richard, M. (2003). *Happiness: A guide to developing life's most important skill*. Boston, MA: Little, Brown.

Rilke, M. (1934/1993). *Letters to a young poet*. New York, NY: Norton.

Rinpoche, S. (1992). *The Tibetan book of living and dying*. San Francisco, CA: Harper.

Ritter, C. (1954/2010). *A woman in the polar night*. Fairbanks, AK: University of Alaska Press.

Sarton, M. (1973). *Journal of a solitude*. New York, NY: Norton.

Seligman, M. (2002). *Authentic happiness: Using the new positive psychology to realize your potential for lasting fulfillment*. New York, NY: Free Press.

Stengel, R. (1995). Space invader. *The New Yorker*, 71, 2–3.

Storr, E. (1988). *On solitude: A return to the self*. New York, NY: Ballantine Books.

Strand, C. (1998). *The wooden bowl: Simple meditations for everyday life*. New York, NY: Hyperion.

Suzuki, S. (2002). *Not always so: Practicing the true spirit of Zen*. New York, NY: Harper Collins.

Thoreau, H. (1853/1997). *The Writings of Henry D. Thoreau. Journal, Volume 5: 1852–1853*. P. F. O'Connell (Ed.). Princeton, NJ: Princeton University Press.

Wallach, J. (1996). *Desert queen: The extraordinary life of Gertrude Bell: Adventurer, adviser to kings, ally of Lawrence of Arabia*. New York, NY: Doubleday.

Werdel, M., & Wicks, R. (2012). *Primer on posttraumatic growth: An introduction and guide*. Hoboken, NJ: Wiley.

Wicks, R. (1992). *Touching the holy: Ordinariness, self-esteem, and friendship*. Notre Dame, IN: Ave Maria Press.

Wicks, R. (1995). *Seeds of sensitivity: Deepening your spiritual life*. Notre Dame, IN: Ave Maria Press.

Wicks, R. (2003). *Riding the dragon: 10 lessons for inner strength in challenging times*. Notre Dame, IN: Sorin Books.

Wicks, R. (2007). *Crossing the desert: Learning to let go, see clearly, and live simply*. Notre Dame, IN: Sorin Books.

Wicks, R. (2008). *The resilient clinician*. New York, NY: Oxford University Press.

Wicks, R. (2010). *Bounce: Living the resilient life*. New York, NY: Oxford University Press.

Williams, M. G., Teasdale, J. D., Segal, Z. V., & Kabat-Zinn, J. (2007). *The mindful way through depression: Freeing yourself from chronic unhappiness*. New York, NY: Guilford Press.

Winnicott, D. (1958). The capacity to be alone. *International Journal of Psycho-analysis, 39*: 416–420.

Bibliography

CLINICIAN SELF-CARE, SECONDARY STRESS, AND RESILIENCY

Baker, E. K. (2002). *Caring for ourselves: A therapist's guide to personal and professional well-being.* Washington, DC: American Psychological Association.

Domar, A. D., & Dreher, H. (2001). *Self-nurture: Learning to care for yourself as effectively as you care for everyone else.* New York, NY: Penguin.

Kottler, J. A. (2003). *On being a therapist.* San Francisco, CA: Wiley.

Leiter, M. P., & Maslach, C. (2005). *Banishing burnout: Six strategies for improving your relationship with work* (3rd ed.). San Francisco, CA: Jossey-Bass.

Pope, K. S., & Vasques, M. J. T. (2005). *How to survive and thrive as a therapist.* Washington, DC: American Psychological Association.

Reinhold, B. B. (1997). *Toxic work: How to overcome stress, overload and burnout and revitalize your career.* New York, NY: Plume.

Reivich, K., & Shatte, A. (2002). *The resilience factor: 7 keys to finding your inner strength and overcoming life's hurdles.* New York, NY: Broadway Books.

Rothschild, B., & Rand, M. (2006). *Help for the helper: The psychophysiology of compassion fatigue and vicarious trauma.* New York, NY: W. W. Norton.

Skovholt, T. M. (2001). *The resilient practitioner: Burnout prevention and self-care strategies for counselors, therapists, teachers, and health professionals.* Boston, MA: Allyn & Bacon.

Weiss, L. (2004). *Therapist's guide to self-care.* New York, NY: Routledge/ Taylor & Francis.

Wicks, R. (2008). *The resilient clinician.* New York, NY: Oxford University Press.

MINDFULNESS

Batchelor, S. (1997). *Buddhism without beliefs*. New York, NY: Riverhead.

Beck, C. (1989). *Everyday Zen: Love and work*. San Francisco, CA: Harper.

Brach, T. (2003). *Radical acceptance: Embracing your life with the heart of a Buddha*. New York, NY: Bantam Dell.

Brantley, J. (2003). *Calming your anxious mind*. Oakland, CA: New Harbinger.

Brazier, D. (1995). *Zen therapy*. New York, NY: Wiley.

Chodron, P. (2001). *The wisdom of no escape and the path of loving-kindness*. Boston, MA: Shambhala.

Dalai Lama & Cutler, H. (1998). *The art of happiness: A handbook for living*. New York, NY: Riverhead.

Epstein, M. (1995). *Thoughts without a thinker: Psychotherapy from a Buddhist perspective*. New York, NY: Basic Books.

Germer, C., Siegel, R., & Fulton, P. (Eds.). (2005). *Mindfulness and psychotherapy*. New York, NY: Guilford Press.

Goldman, D. (2003). *Destructive emotions: How can we overcome them?* New York, NY: Bantam Dell.

Goldstein, J. (1993). *Insight meditation: The practice of freedom*. Boston, MA: Shambhala.

Goldstein, J., & Kornfield, J. (1987). *Seeking the heart of wisdom*. Boston, MA: Shambhala.

Gunaratana, B. (2002). *Mindfulness in plain English*. Somerville, MA: Wisdom Publications.

Hanh, T. N. (1975/1987). *The miracle of mindfulness*. Boston, MA: Beacon Press.

Hayes, S., Follette, V., & Linehan, M. (Eds.). (2004). *Mindfulness and acceptance: Expanding the cognitive-behavioral tradition*. New York, NY: Guilford Press.

Kabat-Zinn, J. (1990). *Full catastrophe living*. New York, NY: Delacorte Press.

Kabat-Zinn, J. (1994). *Wherever you go, there you are: Mindfulness meditation in everyday life.* New York, NY: Hyperion.

Kabat-Zinn, J. (2005). *Coming to our senses: Healing ourselves and the world through mindfulness.* New York, NY: Hyperion.

Kabat-Zinn, J. (2005). *Guided mindfulness meditation.* Series 1-3 [Compact disc]. P.O. Box 547, Lexington, MA: Stress Reduction CDs and Tapes.

Kabat-Zinn, M., & Kabat-Zinn, J. (1998). *Everyday blessings: The inner work of mindful parenting.* New York, NY: Hyperion.

Kornfield, J. (1993). *A path with heart: A guide through the perils and promises of spiritual life.* New York, NY: Bantam.

Kornfield, J. (2000). *After the ecstasy, the laundry: How the heart grows wise on the spiritual path.* New York, NY: Bantam.

Langer, E. (1989). *Mindfulness.* Cambridge, MA: Da Capo Press.

Linehan, M. (2005). *This one moment: Skills for everyday mindfulness.* Seattle, WA: Behavioral Tech.

Salzberg, S. (1995). *Loving kindness: The revolutionary art of happiness.* Boston, MA: Shambhala.

Stern, D. (2004). *The present moment in psychotherapy and everyday life.* New York, NY: W. W. Norton.

Suzuki, S. (1973). *Zen mind, beginner's mind.* New York, NY: John Weatherhill.

Weiss, A. (2004). *Beginning mindfulness: Learning the way of awareness.* Novato, CA: New World Library.

Wicks, R. (2003). *Riding the dragon.* Notre Dame, IN: Sorin Books.

Wicks, R. (2008). *The resilient clinician.* New York, NY: Oxford University Press.

POSITIVE PSYCHOLOGY

Aspinwall, L. G., & Staudinger, U. M. (Eds.). (2003). *A psychology of human strengths: Fundamental questions and future directions for a positive psychology.* Washington, DC: American Psychological Association.

Baumeister, R. F. (2005). *The cultural animal: Human nature, meaning, and social life.* Oxford, UK: Oxford University Press.

Csikszenthmihalyi, M. (1990). *Flow: The psychology of optimal experience.* New York, NY: Harper Perennial.

Csikszenthmihalyi, M. (1998). *Finding flow: The psychology of engagement with everyday life.* New York, NY: Basic Books.

Czikszenthmihalyi, M., & Csikszentmihalyi, I. S. (Eds.). (2006). *A life worth living: Contributions to positive psychology.* New York, NY: Oxford University Press.

Emmons, R. A., & McCullough, M. E. (Eds.). (2004). *The psychology of gratitude.* Oxford, UK: Oxford University Press.

Fowers, B. J. (2005). *Virtue and psychology: Pursuing excellence in ordinary practices.* Washington, DC: American Psychological Association.

Gilbert, D. (2006). *Stumbling on happiness.* New York, NY: Alfred A. Knopf.

Haidt, J. (2006). *The happiness hypothesis: Finding modern truth in ancient wisdom.* New York, NY: Basic Books.

James, W. (2002). *The varieties of religious experience: A study in human nature.* New York, NY: Modern Library.

Keyes, C. L. M., & Haidt, J. (2002). *Flourishing: Positive psychology and the life well-lived.* Washington, DC: American Psychological Association.

Linley, P. A., & Joseph, A. (Eds.). (2004). *Positive psychology in practice.* Hoboken, NJ: Wiley.

Maslow, A. H. (1968/1999). *Toward a psychology of being* (3rd ed.). New York, NY: Wiley.

Norem, J. K. (2001). *The positive power of negative thinking.* Cambridge, MA: Basic Books.

Pearsall, P. (2003). *The Beethoven factor: The new positive psychology of hardiness, happiness, healing, and hope.* Charlottesville, VA: Hampton Roads.

Peterson, C. (2006). *A primer in positive psychology.* New York, NY: Oxford University Press.

Peterson, C., & Seligman, M. E. P. (Eds.). (2004). *Character strengths and virtues: A handbook and classification.* Oxford, UK: American Psychological Association & Oxford University Press.

Seligman, M. E. P. (1990/1998). *Learned optimism: How to change your mind and your life.* New York, NY: Pocket Books.

Seligman, M. E. P. (1993). *What you can change . . . and what you can't: The complete guide to successful self-improvement.* New York, NY: Ballantine Books.

Seligman, M. E. P. (2002). *Authentic happiness: Using the new positive psychology to realize your potential for lasting fulfillment.* New York, NY: Free Press.

Snyder, C. R., & Lopez, S. J. (Eds.). (2002). *Handbook of positive psychology.* Oxford, UK: Oxford University Press.

Permissions

I would like to gratefully acknowledge permission to include material in *The Inner Life of the Counselor* from the following publications:

- Wicks, R. (2008). *The Resilient Clinician*. New York: Oxford University Press, pp. 76–79; Self-Care Protocol Questionnaire for Clinicians.
- Excerpt from *Crossing the Desert* by Robert Wicks. Copyright 2007. Used with permission of the publisher, Ave Maria Press, Inc., P.O. Box 428, Notre Dame, IN 46556, www.avemariapress.com
- Excerpt from *Prayerfulness* by Robert Wicks. Copyright 2009. Used with permission of the publisher, Ave Maria Press, Inc., P.O. Box 428, Notre Dame, IN 46556, www.avemariapress.com

Acknowledgments

I would like to thank Oxford University Press for allowing me to use a table from my book published with them, *The Resilient Clinician*. Similarly, I am grateful to Sorin Books for giving me permission to adapt material on humility and a chapter on being mentored from my book on the desert *Ammas* and *Abbas* entitled *Crossing the Desert* and to adapt material on mindfulness from my book *Prayerfulness: Awakening to the Fullness of Life*.

Stories and anecdotes are a trademark of both my writing and presentations because they are able to capture and communicate in a way that they are often remembered. With this in mind, I would like to thank Jamie Hanner, Gershon Sonnenschein, and Brendan Geary for sharing with me reflections and stories that helped bring my point across in helpful ways.

To my Graduate Research Assistant, Tina C. Buck, I am also indebted for her fine editing of the manuscript. I am truly fortunate since she has both a fine knowledge of the area and superb writing skills. Thank you for your help and recommendations.

An enthusiastic voice from the beginning was Wiley's Executive Editor for Psychology, Patricia "Tisha" Rossi. It is an immeasurable gift when your editor is able to believe in your idea, help you make it the best it can be, and then ensure that everything possible is done to get the word out about it. I am privileged to join all the fine authors she has brought to Wiley because of who she is and how she is able to appreciate the contributions that different books can make across the spectrum of the behavioral sciences.

As always, I have a deep sense of gratitude for my wife, Michaele. Her keen inspiration, amazing patience, and faithful encouragement make my completion of projects such as these a reality. Thank you.

Author Index

Subject Index

197